MW00963490

Suburban Modern

Suburban Modern

Postwar Dreams in Calgary

Robert M. Stamp

Library and Archives Canada Cataloguing in Publication
Stamp, Robert M., 1937-
Suburban modern / Robert M. Stamp.
Includes bibliographical references.
ISBN 1-894898-25-7
1. Suburban life--Alberta--Calgary--History--20th century.
2. Calgary Suburban Area (Alta.)--History--20th century. I. Title.
FC3697.4.S72 2004   306'.09712'33809045 C2004-904393-5

TouchWood Editions acknowledges the financial support for its publishing
program from the Government of Canada through the Book Publishing Industry
Development Program (BPIDP), the Canada Council for the Arts, and the Province
of British Columbia through the British Columbia Arts Council.

We would be grateful for information that would allow us to correct, in a reprint-
ing, any errors or omissions regarding reprinted copyright protected materials
herein.

TouchWood Editions Ltd.
406, 13th Avenue NE
Calgary, Alberta T2E 1C2
www.touchwoodeditions.com
Distributed by
Heritage House
#108-17665-66A Avenue
Surrey, BC, Canada V3S 2A7
greatbooks@heritagehouse.ca
www.heritagehouse.ca

04 05 06 07/6 5 4 3 2 1   Printed in Canada

Contents

introduction
Modern Pioneers 6
chapter 1
Waiting for the Modern Age 11
chapter 2
A Vertical Downtown 29
chapter 3
A City Built for Speed 51
chapter 4
The Postwar Dream House 83
chapter 5
Through Subdivision Sprawl to Seamless City 115
chapter 6
Living the Modern Life 143
chapter 7
The Limits of Modernism 171

endnotes 194
suggestions for further reading 202
author Information 208

introduction

Modern Pioneers

When Arlene and I returned to Calgary in the summer of 1995—back in the city after a 12-year absence—we moved into a modest postwar house in Parkdale. Built and first occupied in the early 1950s, the house is a three-bedroom, flat-roof back-split—a model popular at that time in new suburban areas. Though upgraded and added to in the mid-80s, the house remains true to the spirit and style of what I have labelled "suburban modern"— the aesthetic that dominated Calgary development in the quarter century following the Second World War and that remains a defining feature of today's sprawling 1,000,000-strong city.

Intrigued by both the interior and exterior look of our house, and other houses on the block, I became interested in the beginnings and early development of our immediate neighbourhood. My research took me back to April 1950, when surveyor R.M. McCutcheon trod through the grassy field on the north bank of the Bow River, measuring the land, marking out streets and property lines. Under McCutcheon's eyes and hands, our block was mathematically divided into 10 lots on the east side, most 45 by 120 feet (13.7 by 36.6 metres), and 11 lots on the west side, most 48 by 108.8 feet (14.6 by 33.2 metres).

House builders came next, led by Nu-West, bringing bull-

dozers, truckloads of lumber, power tools and work crews. Up
went standard one-storey and storey-and-a-half Wartime Housing
models, still being built in the first few years of peacetime. There
were also early examples of the Calgary Bungalow school, one-
storey houses set horizontally against the street and marked by
strong horizontal bands of coloured clapboard with stucco above.
Split-level, flat-top houses, both side-splits and back-splits, also
gave our block, and neighbouring blocks to the east and west, a
distinctive look.

Residents quickly moved in and took possession of these
dwellings. The 1951 *City of Calgary Directory* shows 13 of the
block's 21 properties occupied, while the eight remaining houses
were claimed over the next four years. Some of these Parkdale
pioneers came from older Calgary neighbourhoods, while others
were newcomers to the city. Were they attracted to our block
because of its proximity to the river? Did they like the easy access
to downtown along Parkdale Boulevard and Bowness Road? Or
did 15 years of pent-up housing demand simply propel these
pioneers to the nearest available lots and homes?

Culturally, these early residents were not very diverse.
Judging by city directories from the 1950s, 39 of the block's 58
families during its first decade bore Anglo-Celtic surnames, with
the remaining households a mix of French, German, Scandinavian
and Slavic names. Yet residents varied considerably in occupational
status. Far from the homogeneity expected of a postwar suburb,
the street presented a mix of bosses and employees, hourly wage-
earners and self-employed professionals—including salespersons,
managers, a corporate vice-president, mechanics and machinists, a
carpenter and an electrician, a postmistress and a teacher, a claims
adjuster and an oilfield scout.

Soon sidewalks were laid and the street was paved. Before
the end of the decade, residents welcomed a school and a
community centre to the north, but were less than enthusiastic

about the Cinema Park Drive-In movie theatre to the west. Twenty years later they cheered as the drive-in gave way to Point McKay's upscale condominium development. During the 1980s, they fought off a six-lane expressway along the north bank of the Bow River, and settled for an upgraded jogging and cycling path. Entering the third millennium, they coped with nearby monster-house and large-scale condominium development, and shed a tear as declining enrollment forced the Calgary Board of Education to close their school.

After absorbing Parkdale's origins and subsequent develop-ment as a "suburban modern" neighbourhood, I expanded my reading and research on the city of Calgary. I focussed on the years from the end of the Second World War in 1945 to about 1967, the year of Canada's Centennial and Expo '67 in Montreal. I browsed through old issues of the *Calgary Herald* and various magazines and journals, and sampled records at the Glenbow Archives, the City of Calgary Archives and the University of Calgary Archives. It seemed obvious that Calgary moved in particular architectural and aesthetic directions during those first two postwar decades, resulting in a look and feel I have dubbed "suburban modern."

Before long, I found myself part of a group of city architects and architectural historians, planning an exhibit called "Calgary Modern: 1947–1967." The show attracted considerable interest and attention during its early 2000 run at the Nickle Arts Museum, University of Calgary. The accompanying catalogue included my essay titled "Suburban Modern: Looking for an Aesthetic in Postwar Calgary." So thanks to Douglas Gillmor, chair of the Calgary Modern Advisory Committee, and to committee members Marc Boutin, Linda Cunningham, Ann Davis, Gerald Forseth, Jane Kondo, Michael McMordie, Geoffrey Simmins and Jeremy Sturges, for their inspiration and their tolerance of my down-scale, middle-class, somewhat "subversive" approach to modernism.

Douglas Gillmor subsequently put me in contact with TouchWood Editions. When they suggested that I expand my original catalogue essay into a full-length book on Calgary modernism, I jumped at the opportunity. Here then, with thanks to those individuals and institutions mentioned above, is a look at postwar Calgary, a look at an aesthetic I have christened "suburban modern," a look at how today's city got its streamlined look.

Robert M. Stamp
Calgary, Alberta
August 2004

chapter 1

Waiting for the Modern Age

Hello Calgary!

The Modern Age came late to Calgary. While avant-garde, adversarial modernism disrupted the art salons, architecture schools and design academies of the world's more sophisticated urban centres, Calgary slept through the cultural upheavals of the early 20th century as a provincial backwater, a late-Victorian imperial outpost on the northwest frontier of an artistic wasteland. True, Calgary flourished during the pre-First World War era. As settlers moved west, the community's population mushroomed, and the city became the commercial centre for southern Alberta. But Calgarians paid more attention to subdivision development than to European cultural experimentation. They read their papers for news of fortunes made or lost in cattle or oil, rather than for esoteric reviews of New York's 1913 Armoury Show.

Nor did modernism make any significant impact on Calgary during the next few decades. The collapse of the land and oil booms, followed by the trauma of the First World War and the generally depressed economy of the interwar years, encouraged intellectual retrenchment rather than experimentation. The city's residential and commercial building of the 1920s went ahead without acknowledging the Bauhaus movement, while the paucity of architectural development during the 1930s contributed to an ignorance of the International Style. At the end of the Depression, Calgarians did not look to the visionary, forward-looking 1939 New York World's Fair for design innovation, but rather to the royal visit of King George VI and Queen Elizabeth as a means of solidifying traditional loyalties.

"Street Scene, Calgary" by W.F. Irwin in *Highlights*, published by the Alberta Society of Artists.

Calgarians put patriotism before modernism, wartime production ahead of consumer luxuries, for the six-year duration of the Second World War. The city's population increased from about 85,000 at the outbreak of the war to just over 100,000 in 1946—an increase of almost 20 percent in seven years. These Calgarians survived food rationing, cramped living quarters and patched-up old cars. With nylon stockings in short supply, young women had painted their legs; when the first big sale of stockings occurred in February 1945, girls young and old mobbed downtown stores. On V-J day in August of that year, some 20,000 exuberant Calgarians jammed into the Stampede Grounds and "frolicked in the glow of a massive bonfire on Scotsman's Hill."[1]

The industrial side of postwar Calgary featured meatpacking and flour milling, the CPR Ogden shops, and modest petroleum refining and distribution from the Turner Valley oil field. Calgary was a quiet little city, writes Allan Connery of 1947:

> Streetcars and horse-drawn milk wagons contended with cars for space on city streets. The main roads were paved, but some side streets were still dirt, graded and oiled every year. The Palliser Hotel and the Robin Hood flour mill loomed over the city skyline. Tuxedo Park, West Hillhurst, Elbow Park and Inglewood were at the edge of the city, with a few scattered houses beyond.[2]

Hardly fertile ground for international modernism!

Yet earlier that year, Ottawa journalist Reginald Hardy had described Calgary as the "friendliest, gayest, most unpredictable city in Canada," with seemingly unlimited potential. "Calgary is still growing," he observed, "popping buttons and bursting the seams of its jacket as it flexes its muscles and grins happily into the future." While acknowledging the salute to the past represented by the Stampede and the Southern Alberta Pioneers' and Old

Timers' Association, Hardy suggested Calgary might better be called "The City of Tomorrow" for it was "to the opportunities that lie ahead that Calgary looks."

> And because her people are full of zip and go, because they are ready to take a chance on a cattle deal, a new oil well, a gamble in wheat, or anything else for that matter, it is a city that exudes a healthy spirit of enterprise and adventure ... [Calgarians'] trust in the future and in their ability to make the most of it is instinctive and inspiring."[3]

Other writers caught Hardy's enthusiasm. "The altitude—3,489 feet—gives the air an exhilarating quality not unlike a mild intoxication," wrote Robert Stead in the *Canadian Geographic Journal*.

Marion Nicoll, *Prophet*. 1960. (Collection of Glenbow Museum, Calgary, Canada)

"And it is progressive. Calgary has neither fear nor compunction about breaking away from the old and establishing the new."[4] Meanwhile, James Gray felt Calgary's "ebullient, good humoured brashness has somehow touched a spark and ignited something Canadians never even suspected they possessed—an explosive personality."[5]

Still a Long Way To Go

The vast distance between Calgary and the avant-garde modernism of mid-century is illustrated by the city's reaction to shifting movements in the visual arts. *Calgary Herald* reviewer Geneva Lent reacted negatively to a "disturbing exhibition" of "definitely modern" painting by the Canadian Group of Painters at Coste House in early 1945. "It is the kind of show which causes consternation in the minds of those who prefer painting of the older schools, where beauty, composition, rationality and pictorial qualities were of first consideration," complained Lent.[6]

Art historians might date modernism's tentative arrival in Calgary to a January day in 1946, when artist Maxwell Bates stepped off a passenger train at the CNR railway station, home after 15 years in Europe.

Maxwell Bates, *Still Life with Orange*. 1960. (Collection of Glenbow Museum, Calgary, Canada. © Estate of Maxwell Bates. Reproduced with permission.)

Bates highlighted a group show at Coste House in June 1948, "undoubtedly the most challenging and exciting exhibition of paintings ever displayed by Western Canadian painters," according to an anonymous *Herald* reviewer. Bates was the first in a series of local artists profiled in the *Herald* in 1953, quoted as believing "that the first mission of an artist is an uncompromising interpretation of life."[7] Yet Bates soon discovered that Calgary's tolerance for modern art remained low. Controversy surrounded the 1957 purchase of a Bates painting by the Allied Arts Centre, and City Council rejected his modernist mural design for the new Calgary airport terminal building.[8]

Although strangers to Maxwell Bates and modern art, most Calgarians of the day considered themselves thoroughly modern, although in a much different sense. At war's end in 1945, city residents patronized the Modern Barber Shop and the Modern Beauty Shoppe in Bridgeland-Riverside, ate at the Modern Café on 8th Avenue SE, got their clothes pressed at Modern Cleaners on Centre Street downtown, and bought new automobiles at Modern Motors on 6th Avenue SW. Over the next few years, they bought new homes through Modern Real Estate, carpeted their floors at Modern Floor Coverings, furnished their rooms at Modern Home Accessories or House of Modern Furniture, painted and papered their walls at Modern Decorators, and tuned into the electronic world through Modern Radio and Television Service. Finally, when the dust built up, they turned to the Modern Building Cleaning Service.

Just what did Calgarians mean when they used the word "modern" so glibly and so widely? Photographer Eric Causton called his premises "Calgary's Most Modern Photographic Studio" simply because it was the city's newest such business. In a New Moon Grocery Store newspaper advertisement, modern meant the "best merchandise at the best value." At J.J. Fitzpatrick's men's wear store, modern implied a "comprehensive knowledge of store design, layout and function," including concealed lighting. At the "completely new and modern" plant of Economy Cleaners and Tailors, modern meant an "up-to-date dry cleaning process" that assured clothes of "careful and expert handling." Maclin Motors called its new service shop modern because of such advanced construction details as fireproofing, hydraulically operated doors and fluorescent lighting fixtures, plus the added bonus of a "modern up-to-date coffee counter."[9]

Given the city's collective fixation with the word "modern," perhaps Calgary-style modernism had already arrived before artist Maxwell Bates returned home in January 1946. Perhaps it reached the city in February 1947 when Imperial Oil blew in its well at Leduc, propelling Calgary from regional branch-plant to international-headquarters status in the petroleum business. In

November 1948, Tom Brooks and Les Lear wrapped the Calgary Stampeders football team around an innovative and modernist-looking T-formation backfield to cap an undefeated season with a Grey Cup victory. Or did modernism arrive gradually through the postwar years as Calgarians embraced coloured margarine and

Advertisement, May 16, 1950. *(The Calgary Herald)*

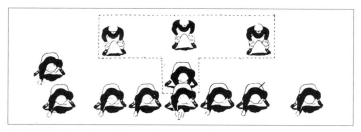

The T-formation adopted by coach Les Lear of the Calgary Stampeders for the 1948 season. *(The Calgary Herald)*

mixed drinking, parking meters and fluoridated water, Sunday sport and drive-in movies?

Local movie theatres linked themselves inextricably with modernism. With its new entrance and marquee in 1949, the

Some of the thousands of Calgarians who jammed mixed drinking establishments in the city in 1958 for their first taste of liquor in public, with the women seen leaving premises through doorways marked "Ladies & Escorts." (Glenbow Archives NA–2864–4009; NA–2864–4009–1a)

downtown Grand Theatre was "one of the most modern in Canada," while the renovated Plaza in the Kensington neighbourhood was an "ultra-modern theatre." In March 1951, the Uptown in the new Barron Building opened as "one of the most modern motion picture theatres in the country," with "its spacious and curving foyer, its lobby and mezzanine painted in warm pastel tones and illuminated with indirect lighting."[10]

Most modern of all were the suburban drive-in movie theatres that catered to the automotive culture of the postwar era. Chinook Park Drive-In opened in 1949 on a 15-acre tract of land on Macleod Trail that later housed Chinook Centre. Boasting a 50 by 47-foot screen (15 by 14 meters), the largest in Canada, the drive-in was touted as the "most modern project of its kind in the Dominion." Chinook was followed by the Sunset on Edmonton Trail and Cinema Park on Bowness Road. With the largest car capacity in Canada and the "biggest picture screen ever built for

Advertisement, July 15, 1953. *(The Calgary Herald)*

a drive-in in this country," Cinema Park in 1953 was billed as the "most ambitious effort to date" in Calgary entertainment circles.[11]

Modernism By Any Other Name ...

Everyone uses the word *modern*—even though the word is anything but. It was popularized in the 17th century with the 1631 publication of the book *Architectura Moderna*, which featured the work of Dutch sculptor and architect Hendrik de Keyser, and promoted a new way of thinking about architectural form. A century later, French architect Charles-Etienne Briseux reinforced this thinking with his 1728 book, *L'Architecture Moderne*. Dramatic structures such as London's Crystal Palace (1851) and the Eiffel Tower in Paris (1889) seemed to illustrate modern building, while many technological innovations—the printing press, cotton gin, factory system, steam engine, electricity, radio, satellite, computer—have each in turn been hailed as precipitating the dawn of the modern age.

For Canadian artists, architects and designers, argues Allan Collier, modernism had its roots in Europe at the beginning of the 20th century at a time of rapid industrialization. It developed in response to mass production, which, "for reasons of efficiency, required the removal of extraneous detailing and the abstraction of form into linear and geometric components." Through the 1920s, "an awareness of the power of the machine to transform life" led to much experimentation in architecture and design in anticipation of a new age. In France, architectural visionary Le Corbusier experimented with houses as "machines for living" that incorporated open planning and component furniture, which also became commercially available in Germany in the late 1920s. Instructors and students at the Bauhaus explored the newly emerging role of the industrial designer and produced a limited number of functionalist prototypes for mass production.[12]

Richard Craig and Jim Smith mark the end of an era with the final home ice delivery, September 30, 1961. (Glenbow Archives NA–2864–672)

Yet for most Canadians, certainly the majority of Calgarians, modernism remained a rather foreign cultural construct, associated with avant-garde art and architecture. Yet it soon crossed the Atlantic with the ease and speed of modern transoceanic steamships. The New York Armory show of 1913 used the word to describe controversial paintings by Henri Matisse and Pablo Picasso. By 1925, "modern" attached itself to the avant-garde style introduced at the Paris Art Deco show. In 1929 it was legitimized with the opening of the Museum of Modern Art (MOMA) in New York. The term acquired a certain middle-class acceptance with the "World of Tomorrow" theme of the 1939 New York World's Fair.

Mid-century *modern* continued apace as Calgary gradually became comfortable with the term. The movement's centre, however, remained in the art and architectural worlds of far-away New York with Jackson Pollock's painting *Echo: Number 25* in 1951, Mies van der Rohe's Seagram Building of 1958, and Andy Warhol's painting *Twenty Marilyns* in 1962. By the late 1960s, however, most Calgarians could share in the excitement of such epic modern adventures as Montreal's Expo '67, featuring Buckminster Fuller's geodesic dome, and Neil Armstrong and Buzz Aldrin landing on the moon in 1969. Yet the Modern Age had a limited shelf life, for by the mid-1970s architect and critic Charles Jencks had begun popularizing the term postmodern.

But what is "modern"? And how modern is the term itself? The Oxford English Dictionary traces the word to the Latin *modernus* and the French *moderne*, working its way into mid-16th-century English as "just now" or "of today." Over the next 350 years, the word acquired a host of meanings. As a noun, modern came to signify someone living in or belonging to the present time, one belonging to a modern as contrasted with an older period, one whose tastes or opinions are up-to-date, or someone belonging to the so-called modern school of thought in relation to a subject.

"Modern" is even more attractive as an adjective: of or pertaining to the present and recent times, as distinguished from the remote past; pertaining to or originating in the current age or period; belonging to a comparatively recent period in the life-history of the world; that which is modern or peculiar to modern times; of a movement in art and architecture, or the works produced by such a movement; characterized by a departure from or a repudiation of accepted or traditional styles and values; characteristic of the present and recent times; new-fashioned; not antiquated or obsolete; everyday, ordinary, commonplace.

"Modern" thrives as well in various specialty phrases: a modern convenience suggests an amenity, device or fitting such as

CBC-TV studio, February 6, 1961. (Glenbow Archives NA–5093–939)

is usual in a modern house; modern dance implies a free expressive style of dancing distinct from classical ballet; modern jazz denotes jazz of a type which originated during and after the Second World War; a modern first is an antiquarian bookseller's term for the first edition of a book published after about 1900.

"Modern" also spawned many derivatives. The word "modernist" emerged in the 1580s signifying a supporter or follower of modern ways and methods; or someone who advocates the teaching of modern languages rather than the ancient classics; or an artist, architect or writer whose work is characterized by modern traits. During the 1620s, "modernity" entered the language to signify the quality or condition of being modern, modernness of character or something that is modern.

Then came "modernism" in the 1730s to denote a usage, mode of expression, or peculiarity of style or workmanship, characteristic of modern times; modern character or quality of thought, expression or style of workmanship; sympathy with

Advertisement, May 18, 1954. *(The Calgary Herald)*

or affinity to what is modern; a tendency or movement toward modifying traditional beliefs and doctrines in accordance with the findings of modern criticism and research; the methods, style or attitude of modern artists; a style of painting, architecture, literature or music in which the artist deliberately breaks away from classical and traditional methods of expression.

By the 1740s, English-speaking peoples begin using the word "modernize" for making or rendering modern, giving a modern character or appearance to, bringing about modern conditions in, or especially remodeling and refashioning older buildings. By the 1770s, the lexicon is completed when the word "modernization" is used to describe the action or act of modernizing or the state of being modernized.

Despite shelves full of dictionaries and seminar rooms

packed with squabbling academics, terms such as modern, modernist, modernism and modernize all remain decidedly ambiguous. They can be used in a very specific sense, referring to the series of radical movements in the arts that culminated in the early decades of the 20th century. For our purposes, perhaps a more general sense is appropriate, referring to modern attitudes and a modern consciousness—including a readiness for change, an interest in the fashionable and the contemporary, and a broadly secular, materialist outlook—that gripped Calgarians in the 20 to 25 years following the Second World War.

Being Modern

To be modern, argues cultural critic Marshall Berman, is to find ourselves in an environment that "promises us adventure, power, joy, growth, transformation of ourselves and the world—and at the same time threatens to destroy everything we have, everything we know, everything we are." Modern environments and experiences "cut across all boundaries of geography and ethnicity, of class and nationality, or religion and ideology; in this sense modernity can be said to unite all mankind." But it is a paradoxical unity, claims Berman, a unity of disunity; it "pours us all into a maelstrom of perpetual disintegration and renewal, of struggle and contradiction, of ambiguity and anguish." To be modern is to be part of a universe in which, as Marx said, "all that is solid melts into air."

In the 20th century, continues Berman, the social processes that brought this maelstrom into being, and kept it in a state of perpetual becoming, have come to be called "modernization." These world-historical processes have nourished an amazing variety of visions and ideas that aim to make men and women the "subjects as well as the objects of modernization, to give them the power to change the world that is changing them, to make their way through the maelstrom and make it their own."[13] As John Wilson Foster maintains:

> Modernism was in most countries an extraordinary compound of the futuristic and the nihilistic, the revolutionary and the conservative, the naturalistic and the symbolic, the romantic and the classical. It was a celebration of a technological age and a condemnation of it; an excited acceptance of the belief that the old regimes of culture were over, and a deep despairing in the face of that fear; a mixture of convictions that the new forms were escapes from historicism and the pressures of the time with convictions that they were precisely the living expressions of these things.[14]

In many ways, 20th-century modernism thrived and grew beyond its own wildest hopes. In painting and sculpture, in poetry and the novel, in theatre and dance, in architecture and design, in a whole array of electronic media and in a wide range of scientific disciplines that did not exist 100 years earlier, the century produced an amazing array of works and ideas of the highest quality. And yet, cautioned Berman in 1982, "we don't know how to use our modernism; we have missed or broken the connection between our culture and our lives ... We have mostly lost the art of putting ourselves in the picture, of recognizing ourselves as participants and protagonists in the art and thought of our time." While the century "nourished a spectacular modern art," we seem to have "forgotten how to grasp the modern life from which this art springs."[15]

While Berman and Foster speak to an international, avant-garde audience, writer Suzi Gablik brings modernism closer to the experience of the average postwar Calgarian when she highlights its secular nature. By secularism, Gablik implies nothing less than the "de-spiritualization of the world, the modernist refusal of the sacred." It refers to the rationalizing process, tributary to the development of science and technology, "through which the numinous, the mythic, and the sacramental have been, in our society, reduced to rags"; and the gradual triumph, under advanced "late" capitalism, of a "bureaucratic, managerial type of culture characterized by mass consumption and economic self-seeking."[16]

Modernism is also a largely urban phenomenon. The city is where modernity and modernism happened. Separate aspects of the city, argues British critic John Jervis, "both coalesce and pull apart: the city is rational project, and the excess of theatricality; it is pleasure and danger, a site of moral conflict; fragmented yet interconnected; monolithic, yet heterogeneous; masculine and feminine. It is a place of fluidity and diversity, rather than rootedness and community, yet simultaneously reproduces communities within itself." Conventionally, the modern city, with its sleek buildings, its streamlined streets, can be presented as a hymn to rationality, a key exemplar of the project of modernity. The modernization of the city, continues Jervis, has been an attempt to "impose a rational form on an inchoate mass, and thereby produce a city that would be intelligible, legible."[17]

As urban Calgarians embraced the Modern Age in the years following the Second World War, they redefined terms such as "modern" and "modernism." They shifted the emphasis from high modernism to a secular, mass-market modernism, from capital-M to small-m modernism. They moved modernism out of the studios of the avant-garde producers and into the hands (and hearts) of middle-class consumers, out of downtown art salons and design studios and onto the streets and into the suburbs. They went beyond modern art, modern architecture and modern design, and redefined modernism to include modern homes in modern suburbs, with modern furniture and modern appliances and modern cars. For postwar Calgarians, modernism meant personal betterment, achieving all those material gains that had been delayed or denied by 15 years of depression and war.

Calgarians democratized, feminized and suburbanized modernism.

North Hill Shopping Centre, April 1, 1959. (Glenbow Archives NA–2864–1854–B–ix)

chapter 2

A Vertical Downtown

The Yanks are Coming

Oil and gas people date the arrival of the modern era in Calgary on February 13, 1947, when Imperial Oil blew in its famous well at Leduc, some 250 kilometers (155 miles) north of the city. That day, Imperial was probing the Devonian Reef formation with Leduc No. 1, its 134th well since 1914. Suddenly the afternoon sky was filled with belching flame and dense black smoke. Imperial's 133-hole drought had ended, and the "lid was finally lifted off the enormous oil and natural gas reserves of Western Canada."[1] LEDUC WELL ROARS IN WITH OIL headlined the next morning's *Albertan*, confirming the beginning of a new era in the city's development.

Western Examiner, February 22, 1947. (Glenbow Archives NA–789–80)

Follow-up drilling proved remarkably successful; 131 of the 147 wells drilled in the Leduc area in 1948 became producers. The greatest Alberta oil boom was underway and the "whole structure of the postwar Alberta economy began to alter."[2] Before Leduc, the petroleum industry was responsible for less than two percent of personal income generated in the province. Within four years the industry generated more than one quarter of that income, and by the mid-1950s it was responsible for 45 percent, replacing agriculture at the top of the list.[3]

Growth of the Alberta Petroleum Industry [4]			
	1947	1960	1972–74
Capable oil wells in Alberta	502	9,878	14,168
Annual production of crude oil in barrels	6.3m	133.5m	522.2m
Money spent in exploration	$25m	$353m	$870m
Cubic feet of natural gas	48m		2,613m

Leduc's success could hardly have come at a more opportune time for Calgary. Production from the Turner Valley field just south of Calgary had begun to decline, prairie consumption was increasing, and Calgary oil refineries, argues David Breen, were on the verge of arranging crude oil imports from the United States. But with Leduc, Alberta suddenly became an oil surplus region again. The location of existing refineries, plus Calgary's status as headquarters of most oil companies operating in the west, gave the city an initial advantage that suggested its "continued pre-eminence as administrative and financial centre of the Canadian petroleum industry."[5]

Head offices and branch offices of major Canadian and American oil and gas firms consolidated their management, financial and strategic decision-making operations in Calgary. City office buildings also housed independent operators: investment

Eaton's store, 1945. (Glenbow Archives NA–2304–1)

firms and oil brokers; geological, geophysical and engineering consultants; lease brokers and land agents; data processing and petroleum publishing firms. Calgary companies directly involved with the petroleum industry mushroomed from 133 in 1946 to 2,130 in 1974, giving the city more than 50 percent of all oil and gas head offices in Canada. By the mid-1960s, Calgary's association with the oil and gas industry gave it the third highest number of head offices in the country.[6]

Meanwhile, companies specializing in oilwell drilling, oilfield construction and servicing, pipelines and transportation, and service and repair shops expanded activities in the city's industrial areas, beginning with the 240-acre (97-hectare) Manchester Industrial District off Macleod Trail SE in 1954.

Industrial parks offered relatively inexpensive tracts of serviced land, and road transport into them offered an alternative to rail for goods and to public transit for workers. These parks featured modernist-style, single-storey industrial buildings, which were cheaper to build per square foot of construction than multi-storey buildings, provided a higher percentage of usable floor space, and allowed more flexible layouts and more efficient flows of goods, thus lowering production costs.[7] By 1958, the city had also developed Highfield Industrial Park, while Bonnybrook, North Calgary, Ogden-Barlow and Meridian industrial parks were being privately developed.

The overriding reason for petroleum firms clustering in Calgary, claims G.H. Zieber, was their "desire to be near other oil companies." Although producers, explorers and developers were highly competitive, they were also characterized by a large number of joint ventures or shared activities. American and international oil people coming into Alberta gravitated to Calgary "to make contacts and find out what was happening" in the industry. Executives and managers, prospectors and consultants "got to know each other in Calgary." They fraternized through clubs, especially the Calgary Petroleum Club, launched in 1948 by American and Canadian oilmen, thus establishing strong business and social ties.[8]

Calgary was closer to the United States than Edmonton, and it offered better air connections and an entrepreneurial orientation that appealed to American oilmen and oil investors. No doubt the physical and cultural environment of southern Alberta, and the spirit of Calgary characterized by ranching, cowboys and the annual Stampede, was also attractive to American oilmen because it was similar to what they had known in Texas and Oklahoma.

In 1946, fewer than 100,000 people lived in Calgary. By 1965, the figure stood at 315,680 and represented an annual increase of over 5.8 percent; in 1971, the population topped 400,000.

Welcome sign, late 1940s. (Glenbow Archives NA–3539–17)

Historian Max Foran identifies three crucial features of this population explosion: the peculiar nature of the work force, more white-collar oriented and affluent than in typical Canadian metropolitan centres; the superimposition of a sizeable prairie immigrant population onto a relatively small nucleus of Calgary-born residents; and the solidification of an American influence long observable in the city.

Calgary is probably the most "Americanized" of all Canadian cities, concluded Foran in 1978. "Strong north-south links have been traditional since the days of the open range." Calgary's association with the petroleum industry "accentuated this strong liaison with the United States." By 1965, over 30,000 Americans lived in the city, with their numbers directed toward the higher income brackets. They figured prominently in the city's social and economic life, and in many ways Calgary had "more in common with Tulsa or Houston than with Toronto, Montreal or Hamilton."[9]

This Yankee invasion followed quickly on the heels of the Leduc discovery. During 1948, 1949 and 1950, recalls writer James Gray, "Americans were pouring into Alberta, particularly Calgary, by the thousands." Well-service, drilling and geophysical companies "clogged the highways with their massive convoys of equipment" from as far south as Texas and Louisiana. Technical

Mayor Don Mackay, 1950–59. (Glenbow Archives NA–2775–1)

specialists like geophysicists, drilling mud purveyors and "every type of engineer known to the industry" scoured the town for office space. On a five-minute walk from the Palliser Hotel, "you would encounter accents ranging from Louisiana patois to Texas drawl, New England twang, and upper crust English."

Along with the American drilling rigs, draw-works, well-head fittings and drill pipe by the carload, continues Gray, came a steadily increasing influx of "eager-beaver junior executives on their way to the top," enthusiastically seizing "their first opportunity to test their upward mobility on their companies' executive ladders." In Alberta they filled the top executive and supervisory positions of the American branch offices. Meanwhile, Calgary "broke out in a rash of American licence plates, American cigarettes, and American Stetsons."[10]

Americans who came to Alberta in the postwar era had a notable social and political impact. In the early years of the boom, most senior management of the major oil companies, largely American-owned, were from California, Oklahoma, Texas and Louisiana. From 1955 to 1970, nine of 15 presidents of Calgary's exclusive Petroleum Club were Americans. Faced with growing pressure from Canadians in their ranks, and aware of growing nationalism, American oil companies gradually Canadianized their personnel during the 1960s. The Americans who remained usually took out Canadian citizenship so they could vote. Like their counterparts in the United States, they imported both their strong right-wing views and an enthusiasm for involvement in voluntary organizations.[11]

The postwar construction industry was barely back in business when the American influx hit. House builders could not keep up with the burgeoning demand from incoming Americans. Undeterred by the housing scarcity, writes Gray, American oil companies "simply opened their purse-strings and sent their agents into Calgary's Mount Royal district to buy up the most luxurious houses available for their top executives, eight or ten units at a time."[12]

Building the Towers

The physical impact of the oil industry was even more startling and significant than the demographic change. Downtown Calgary was dramatically transformed between the mid-1940s and the late 1960s, as early 20th century sandstone structures were replaced with towering multi-storied edifices that housed Imperial, Shell, Gulf, Texaco, Pacific Petroleum, Home and other oil companies. Yet change did not happen overnight. When Imperial's Leduc Number One came in, cautions architectural historian Trevor Boddy, a great deal of uncertainty was created in the city. Not only was office space in short supply in Calgary, but Edmonton officials, keen to attract business to their city, broadcast to oil company executives the advantages of locating their offices closer to the new fields and planned refineries.[13]

While Calgary newspapers boasted the announcement of a new office building almost every week during 1948, by the end of 1949 none had even been started. One such project was the Oil Centre Building, touted with great fanfare for the northwest corner of 7th Avenue and 2nd Street SW in the heart of Calgary's business district. Promoted by New Yorker Strabo Claggett and his Whitney-Phoenix Corporation, the 16-storey building would be "Calgary's biggest and most modern." Yet high construction costs and other factors upset the plan. Within a year the site was sold to Royalite Oil Company and eventually became the site for the Royalite Building.[14]

At this point, Calgary lawyer and theatre owner J.B. Barron sensed a perfect opportunity for the bold, mixed-use office tower and cinema complex he had long wanted to build. Barron convinced Great West Life Assurance Company to grant a mortgage of $850,000 on a stylistically unusual design by Calgary architect Jack Cawston. Plans for the $1,250,000, 11-storey office tower "designed along simple, modernistic lines," were announced

Uptown Theatre/Barron Building. (Glenbow Archives NA–5093–247)

in February 1949. Despite technical problems and the lack of a major tenant, Larwill Construction company began work later that year, a particularly bold move, asserts Boddy, "given the then tenuous state of the oil industry in western Canada, and, hence, the uncertainty of the continuing presence of the industry's largely American upper management."[15]

Opened in May 1951, the Barron Building at 612–8th Avenue SW was the first major postwar building to respond to the demand for office space. The structure featured retail spaces and the Uptown movie theatre on the ground floor, a theatre balcony and restaurant on the mezzanine level, office space on the upper floors and a residence for owner J.B. Barron in the penthouse. Barron's suite opened onto a rooftop garden with lawn, flowers and a water hydrant for his Highland terrier "Butch." The garden won the Vincent Massey Award for excellence in urban planning.

The Uptown was the first new movie theatre in Calgary since 1921, although Barron himself had a longstanding interest in cinemas. In 1948, he poured $50,000 into upgrading his Grand Theatre, one of six movie houses in downtown Calgary. The new entrance and marquee would make the Grand "one of the most modern in Canada." The marquee boasted coloured plastic letters instead of standard black to proclaim current movies. The new floor in the foyer, constructed of terrazzo, coloured with special "fast" colors imported from Seattle, was one of the "first examples of terrazzo decorated with floral rather than geometric designs."[16]

The Barron Building's Uptown, however, "one of the most modern motion picture theatres in the country," would outdo the Grand. The Uptown had a 1000-seat theatre, a spacious and curving foyer, and a lobby and mezzanine painted in warm pastel tones and illuminated with indirect lighting. The *Herald* marvelled at its "unusually large foyer allowing freedom of movement to patrons ... a grand staircase to the mezzanine floor ... more comfortable seats, indirect lighting, and a 'floating, hydraulic stage' capable of being lowered and raised." Barron said the Uptown would concentrate on British and Hollywood productions of the more "sophisticated" type while the Grand would continue to feature "action" type movies.[17]

Royalite Building. (Glenbow Archives NA–4952–4)

The structure's exterior was equally dramatic. The Barron Building, argues Boddy, shows the competing strains of Modern architecture in Alberta building after the Second World War. With "surprising success," the building combines the massing and modernistic ornament of the New York Art Deco skyscraper, ribbon windows lifted from the International Style and a Wrightian penthouse. The building is clad in yellow brick, Tyndall limestone and ornamental aluminum. These last two

40

feature angled chevron and scalloped Art Deco decoration. The stepped back or "wedding cake" massing of the building also refers to the New York Art Deco high-rise.[18]

The Barron Building not only played a crucial role in the development of Calgary's oil patch, but also helped re-structure the city's urban form. Original tenants included the Sun Oil Company, Shell and Socony Mobil, representing a good proportion

Triad Building. (Glenbow Archives NA–5093–659)

of Calgary's major oil business. Within 15 years of the building's opening, petroleum profits and foreign investment money led to such temples of modern business as the Royalite Building at 7th Avenue and 2nd Street in 1955; the Imperial Oil Building at 6th Avenue and 4th Street in 1964; Elveden House and Guiness

Complex at the 700-block of 7th Avenue in 1965. Ironically, the location of Barron's building, to the west of downtown Calgary where the major oil companies remain today, "may have done more to preserve Calgary's architectural heritage than years of efforts by planners and politicians." The focus of new development in west downtown took pressure off the old core in the east end.[19]

Impressed by Jack Cawston's work on the Barron Building, Home Oil chief Bob Brown commissioned the architect to design a nine-storey office tower on 6th Avenue. Completed in 1955, the Brown Building was clad in Manitoba Tyndall stone, with crisply detailed blocked window surrounds in the same material. This light grey, easily worked stone was highlighted by bands of

Petro-Chemical Building. (Glenbow Archives NA–5093–201)

Elveden sign: "A Modern Office Building." (Glenbow Archives NA–2864–1399a)

red granite, and the first two storeys on the 6th Avenue elevation were covered in the same material to "temper at pedestrian level the building's undeniable austerity." Although demolished at the height of a later boom, the Brown Building, concludes Boddy, was "one of Alberta's best examples of high International Style office architecture," exhibiting the "cleanness and clarity of intent and execution which marks the best of this style."[20]

Guinness House construction.
(Glenbow Archives NA–2864–1401b)

Two blocks west of the Barron Building, at 805–8th Avenue SW, sits the Petro-Chemical Building, designed by Stevenson & Raines architects. Opened in 1958, it featured "curtain wall" construction, which achieved an all-glass expression, reduced wall thickness and increased rentable floor area. With its clean lines and strict use of high-quality materials, the Petro-Chemical Building stands as one of Calgary's "earliest works of pure Modernism," and one of Western Canada's first glass and steel "curtain wall" structures.[21]

The Bentall Building was next. Completed in 1958, the 10-storey reinforced concrete structure at 444–7th Ave SW, with 246,000 square feet of leasable space, was the largest office building in the city until Elveden House opened in the early 1960s. In later years, the Bentall Building was described as "squatty, old-fashioned and down at the mouth," hunkering down among the sparkling towers, "slump-shouldered with embarrassment." Later known as the Amoco Building, its 1995 owner, Bimcor (Bell Investment Management Corporation) stood ready to "strip the building right back to the concrete structure in order to rebuild it as a glossy new Class A office building in the heart of the city."[22]

Elveden Centre was commissioned by British Pacific Building Limited, a Guinness subsidiary, and designed in part by the architectural firm of Rule, Wynn & Rule. This was Calgary's first "super block" of speculative phased development, comprising three towers linked by a three-storey podium. The main 20-storey tower, Elveden House, was built by Commonwealth Construction Company in 1959-60 at a cost of $5,000,000, and was considered Calgary's first true "skyscraper," towering 263 feet above the sidewalk. The 14-storey east tower, the British American Oil Building, was added in 1960–61 for $4,500,000, and the 15-storey west tower, Guinness House, was added in 1964 for another $5,000,000.

At the cornerstone laying on October 14, 1960, Calgary Mayor Harry Hays called the building a "landmark, a monument and a milestone."[23] Elveden House and the entire Guinness complex stood out in sharp contrast to many modernist neighbours and later competitors. Boddy points to the hexagon design motif featured on panels, pedestrian canopies, lobby walls

Elveden Complex. (Glenbow Archives NA–4952–12)

Elveden Complex plaza level. (Glenbow Archives PA–2854–416)

and even light diffuser boxes. The predominantly green cladding colour and the mosaic harps and angels are "illusions, unusually explicit for a high Modern building, traceable to the Irish source of the Guinness fortune."[24]

Elveden Centre created a critical mass of office space for the west end of downtown, signaling, in Jane Kondo's words, the "development of contemporary corporate images and addresses for Calgary." With such "modern" features as off-street parking, air-conditioning, efficient elevators, curtain-wall construction and abundant natural light, Elveden House was an expression of "efficiency" in the workplace.[25]

Downtown Modern

Large scale construction of office buildings for oil companies and related businesses greatly extended the downtown geographically—especially west along 7th, 8th and 9th avenues, and created a highly built-up, skyscraper-dominated core. Between 1953 and 1962, office space in Calgary's business district almost doubled. By the 1960s, between 600,000 and 700,000 square feet (55,000 to 65,000 square meters) of new office space was absorbed annually in the downtown core, primarily by oil firms. By the end of that decade, the petroleum industry provided direct employment for close to 10 percent of the city's work force, and indirectly accounted for half the total employment.[26]

At the end of the Second World War, downtown Calgary had the highest proportion of aged buildings in the city, many built before 1914 and most unsuitable for new office uses in the postwar era. Through the 1950s and 1960s, residential land use in the downtown core increasingly gave way to commercial space. This trend was accelerated by a June 1958 zoning by-law that raised the ceiling of office buildings from 12 to 20 storeys, providing that the total floor space area did not exceed eight times

Petroleum Row, 9th Avenue SW, 1959. (Glenbow Archives NA–5093–479)

the lot area covered by the building. This change encouraged single-use zoning as a "solution of the modernist movement for urbanism and housing," and "encouraged the already current trend of a skyscraper dominant core."[27] For years to come, Calgary's downtown became an area of transition and upgrading with the construction of new large-scale office buildings and apartments.

Calgary's office-tower architecture of the 1950s and 1960s was decidedly modernist in style, reflecting both the "economic merits of modern construction techniques as it did from the aesthetics of the modern period." The Barron Building, the Petro-Chemical Building and Elveden Centre, structures that best illuminate modernist tendencies, argues Kondo, "all demonstrate the unique relationship between the economic and architectural climate" in Calgary:

Advertisement in *Western Business.*

Modern architecture ... appealed as a means of responding to the rapid and dynamic growth of the urban workplace. On a pragmatic level, the modern palette of lightweight techniques, synthetic modern materials and modularity resulted in economically feasible strategies for creating large office buildings. The skeleton frame allowed a great amount of flexibility for subdividing floor plates for tenants and shortened construction time. The psychological expression of the modern idiom during this postwar period satisfied the need to reflect innovation and confidence in the future, attributes promoted by the corporate mode of business.[28]

Aerial view, 1968. (Glenbow Archives NA–4952–18)

Fellow architect and curator Gerald Forseth echoes these sentiments:

> There was an increasing need to build quickly with flexible interior space, and companies in Calgary easily accepted the modernist concepts of machined materials, dynamic structural systems, speedy construction methods, and simplified layouts and details. They particularly liked the high-speed elevator high-rise building for its prominence, and the thin-skinned glass facades that gave unlimited views to the beautiful and resource-rich surrounding landscape … vaulted Calgary from its previous predominantly Romanesque and Edwardian architectural roots as a small city into the age of Modernism as a large city.[29]

Calgary's office towers of the 1950s and 1960s are representative of the International style. This style is most easily recognized by its use of the module, usually a square or a rectangle, that forms the basis of the building's design. Hard, angular edges, severely plain surfaces and large expanses of glass express a structural system based on a skeleton of steel or reinforced concrete. At its best, "it is a style of subtlety, relying for its beauty upon harmonious proportions and beautifully finished materials; at its worst it is tiresomely repetitious and cheap looking."[30]

The rise of Modern architecture swept away many of the evolving traditions of 2500 years of architectural design, writes Boddy, replacing them with the "slick and efficient architectural technology that now fills our cities." A common element in modernist thought was the desire to break with history, causing many modern architects to seek "the millennium of rational, functional architecture on a new Jerusalem of high-rise blocks, expansive grids and single-use zoning." Architecture, more than the other disciplines, was galvanized and changed forever by

50

modernism. An alliance of new aesthetic, social, technological and intellectual forces swept away such early 20th-century architectural styles as Expressionism, Art Nouveau, the Picturesque, and variations of Beaux-Arts classicism in the rise to stylistic dominance of the Modern Movement. Calgary's rapid growth and urbanization, Boddy concluded in 1987, "coincided almost exactly with the reign of Modern architecture, and its square, bare, functional buildings will dominate ... for the foreseeable future."[31]

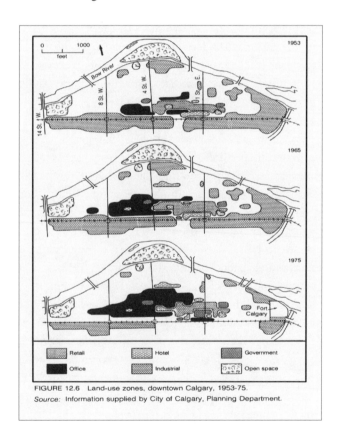

FIGURE 12.6   Land-use zones, downtown Calgary, 1953-75.
Source: Information supplied by City of Calgary, Planning Department.

(Nader. *Cities of Canada.* 1975, 1976.)

chapter 3

A City Built for Speed

Seafoam Green and Oyster White

On June 1, 1947, less than four months after Imperial Oil's Leduc strike, modern public transit arrived in Calgary when the city's first trolley buses rolled out on the Crescent Heights route. These new vehicles incorporated the latest postwar modernist and streamlined design features, and they sported the new colours of the Calgary Transit System—exteriors of seafoam green and oyster white, with gold trim and lettering, and light-and-dark-green interiors.

This dramatic change on the Crescent Heights route marked the first step in Calgary's wholesale conversion from streetcars to trolley coaches

First trolley bus crosses the Louise Bridge, 1947.
(Glenbow Archives NA–2891–28)

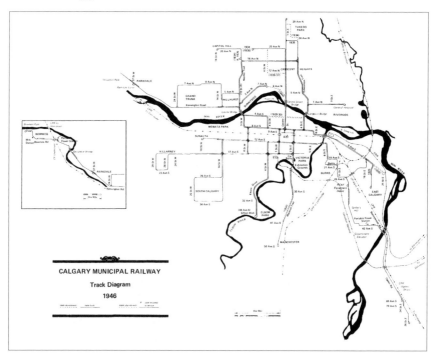

Streetcar track diagram, 1946. (Hatcher, *Stampede City Streetcars.* 1975.)

and gasoline buses during the early postwar years. Between June 1947 and December 1950, all cars of the old Calgary Municipal Railway were replaced and tracks ripped up, as streetcar service throughout the city fell victim to the modernist dictates of postwar public transit. Those policies were first revealed in a report presented to city council in early June of 1945, just four weeks after hostilities ended in Europe. Following a detailed survey of Calgary's transit problems, Toronto-based "urban transportation expert" Norman Wilson recommended "the use of trolley buses in a completely modernized Calgary street railway system."

Like transit planners throughout most of North America, Wilson saw little future in streetcars on rails. Calgary's ancient streetcar fleet should be consigned to the scrap heap, and replaced by a mixed system of trolley, gasoline and diesel buses, with the trolley bus as the main element of the system. The trolley bus provided minimum maintenance, "super-abundance of power" for hill climbing, "rapid and smooth acceleration" and "noiseless and odorless operation," with running costs approximately five cents a mile cheaper than for a gas bus of similar capacity.

Wilson conceded two disadvantages of trolley buses compared to gasoline or diesels: they required overhead wires and offered limited possibilities for charter service. (He omitted any reference to problems caused by route changes or extensions, or of express coaches leap-frogging over local buses!) Wilson did favour gasoline buses on lightly used feeder and suburban routes. Still, the 44-seat trolley bus, with additional room for 30 standees, "has become standardized and is essentially the modern streetcar," he concluded in recommending that trolleys form the backbone of Calgary's postwar transit fleet.[1] That September, council voted overwhelmingly for Wilson's trolley buses, and in January 1946 voters added their support in a city-wide plebiscite.

No one rose up to champion the old, familiar streetcar. First seen on city streets in 1909, the ancient wooden cars of the Calgary Municipal Railway rumbled through the Depression and years of sacrifice occasioned by the Second World War. By 1945, however, after years of neglect, both rolling stock and trackage were in deplorable condition.[2] Collisions and delays seemed almost daily occurrences as the Calgary Herald featured every derailment, however minor, with a front-page picture. There was nothing minor, however, about a January 1946 collision at 14th Street and 17th Avenue SW, when an inbound South Calgary streetcar lost its braking power coming down the 14th Street hill and smashed into a Beltline car at the 17th Avenue intersection. One car was destroyed, the other severely damaged. "Six Calgarians Are Injured/In Runaway Tram Accident" trumpeted the Herald.[3]

Such events played into the hands of local officials. In August 1946, C.V.F. (Vic) Weir was named superintendent of city transit services. Weir was a University of Toronto engineering graduate with previous work experience at Northern Electric, Ontario Hydro and the Edmonton transit system. Weir quickly hired R.H. Wray as chief engineer, with a mandate to convert streetcars to trolley buses. To advance the change even before the conversion program began in earnest, the old Calgary Municipal Railway name was dropped and a new corporate title, Calgary Transit System, was adopted by city council.[4]

Meanwhile, the cars became objects of scorn as citizens looked forward to the arrival of buses. Who wanted clunky old wooden streetcars when streamlined, all-metal trolley coaches and gasoline buses invoked the spirit of the "modern" age? Who would choose to ride on old-fashioned rails when modern rubber-tired vehicles were all the rage? What city council would waste money modernizing its streetcar fleet when there was more economic and more efficient rubber-tired transit available in the postwar era?

In January 1946, city council placed initial orders for Brill "electric trackless trolleys," Brill gasoline buses and GMC diesel hydraulic buses. In November, hundreds of Calgarians took advantage of free rides on the newly arrived trolley coaches. "It's so quiet," was a frequent comment from commuters, accustomed to the rattling of the old streetcars. Others praised the attractive, bright colouring and comfortable seats. Conversion officially began in June 1947, when trolley buses replaced streetcars on the Crescent Heights line. Bus riders and city officials were delighted at the "smooth, almost noiseless mode of electric transportation." Superintendent Weir predicted that "people will walk an extra block or two to travel on a trolley bus instead of a nearby streetcar line."[5]

There was no turning back. By the end of the month, streetcars disappeared from the Capitol Hill and Manchester lines. At year's end, they were gone from Centre Street North and Elbow Drive. Through 1948, trolleys took over the Belt Line, Killarney and South Calgary routes. "Trolley buses have won the whole-hearted approval of the people who use them," exulted the *Calgary Herald* in August 1948. "The big, fast, clean coaches have been successful in every way."[6] The following year, the communities of Bridgeland-Riverside, Sunnyside, Inglewood and Hillhurst said good-bye to their streetcars. Bowness, Montgomery and Parkdale got bus service in April 1950, Burns Avenue in November.

The end for Calgary's rail transit came on December 29, 1950, when Car 14 made the last official farewell run from Ogden into downtown Calgary, completing exactly 38 years of service to the Ogden area and more than 41 years of service in

Last Bowness streetcar leaving downtown, April 1950. (Glenbow Archives NA–2864–1978)

┌─ ━ ━ ━ ━ ━ Clip Out For Future Reference ━ ━ ━ ━ ┐

IMPORTANT NOTICE

CONVERSION
OF
BOWNESS ROUTE
From Street Cars To BUSES

Effective Wednesday morning, April 12th, 1950, transit operation on the Bowness Line will be converted from Street Cars to Buses.

ROUTE. Buses will operate along the present Bowness Road from Bowness to 18th Street N.W., then North to Westmount Road, East to 16th Street N.W., North to Kensington Road, East to 10th Street N.W. and Broadview Boulevard, returning over the same route.

RUSH HOUR SERVICE WILL OPERATE FROM DOWNTOWN

From 6 a.m. to 9 a.m. and from 4 p.m. to 7 p.m. buses will run between Centre Street at 8th Avenue and Bowness.

OFF PEAK SERVICE WILL OPERATE FROM 10TH ST. N.W. ONLY

From 9 a.m. to 4 p.m. and from 7 p.m. to Midnight, patrons going to Bowness will board any one of the following buses in the Centre of the city:—

No. 1 West Calgary, No. 4 Crescent Heights, or No. 9 Sunnyside west bound and transfer to the Bowness bus at 10th Street N.W. and Broadview Boulevard. During the off peak hours east bound patrons will transfer from the Bowness bus at 10th Street N.W. to any of the City bound buses at this point.

NON-STOP SERVICE

Between 10th Street and 25th Street N.W. Bowness buses, west bound, will stop only to pick up passengers for Bowness.

Buses, east bound, will stop only in order to allow passengers to alight.

BOWNESS SCHEDULE
Effective Wednesday, April 12th, 1950.

WEEKDAYS MONDAY TO FRIDAY

Centre St. and 8th Ave.	10th St. N.W.	Bowness
6:00 A.M.	6:10 A.M.	6:30 A.M.
6:15 "	6:25 "	6:45 "
6:30 "	6:40 "	7:00 "
6:45 "	6:55 "	7:15 "
7:00 "	7:10 "	7:30 "
7:07 "	7:17 "	7:45 "
7:22 "	7:32 "	8:00 "
7:37 "	7:47 "	8:15 "
7:52 "	8:02 "	8:30 "
8:15 School Bus	8:27 "	9:00 "
8:22 A.M.	8:32 "	9:00 "
8:52 "	9:00 "	9:30 "

Service from 10th Street N.W. to Bowness

	9:30 A.M.	10:00 A.M.
	10:00 "	10:30 "

and every 30 minutes until 4 p.m. from 10th St. N.W. and Bowness Loop.

4:07 P.M.	4:17 P.M.	4:45 P.M.
4:22 "	4:32 "	5:00 "
4:37 "	4:47 "	5:15 "
4:52 "	5:02 "	5:30 "
5:07 "	5:17 "	5:45 "
5:22 "	5:32 "	6:00 "
5:37 "	5:47 "	6:15 "
5:52 "	6:02 "	6:30 "
6:22 "	6:32 "	7:00 "

Service from 10th St. N.W. to Bowness

	7:00 P.M.	7:30 P.M.
	7:30 "	8:00 "

and every 30 minutes until 11:00 p.m.

11:30 P.M.	12:00 Midnight
12:00 Last Unit	12:30 Last Unit

SATURDAYS ONLY

Centre St. and 8th Ave.	10th St. N.W.	Bowness
6:00 A.M.	6:10 A.M.	6:30 A.M.
6:30 "	6:40 "	7:00 "
6:45 "	6:55 "	7:20 "
7:00 "	7:10 "	7:40 "
7:10 "	7:25 "	8:00 "
8:00 "	8:10 "	8:20 "
8:20 "	8:30 "	8:40 "
		9:00 "

and every 20 minutes until

7:05 P.M	7:15 P.M.	7:45 P.M.
7:30 "	7:40 "	8:10 "
7:55 "	8:05 "	8:35 "
8:20 "	8:30 "	9:00 "
8:45 "	8:55 "	9:25 "
9:10 "	9:20 "	9:50 "
9:35 "	9:45 "	10:15 "

and every 25 minutes until

11:15 P.M.	11:25 P.M.	12:00 Midnight
11:45	11:52 "	12:15 A.M.
12:00 Midnight	12:10 A.M.	12:30 Last Unit

SUNDAYS ONLY

Centre St. 8th Ave.	10th St. N.W.	Bowness
8:30 A.M.		9:00 A.M.
9:30 "		10:00 "
10:00 "		10:30 "
10:30 "		11:00 "
11:00 "		11:30 "
	11:30 A.M.	12:00 Noon

and every 30 minutes until

11:30 P.M.	11:00 P.M.	11:30 P.M.
		12:00 Midnight (Last trip)

For Any Further Information Please Phone M3028

CALGARY TRANSIT SYSTEM

the city. Charles Comba, the driver of Calgary's first streetcar on July 5, 1909, operated the last car for part of its run. A bevy of old Calgarians and civic notables rode the car, led by Mayor Don Mackay. When the car reached 1st Street and 8th Avenue SW, Mackay urged everyone to get out, circle the car and sing *Auld Lang Syne* during the 5:15 p.m. rush hour.[7]

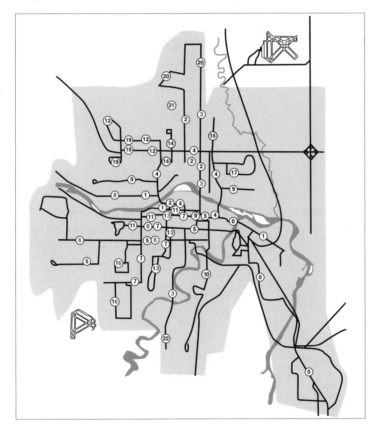

Calgary transit routes 1957. (Glenbow Archives NA–3487–7)

facing page: "Conversion of Bowness Route" notice, 1950. *(The Calgary Herald)*

While gasoline buses took over on Ogden Road, electric trolley coaches hummed smoothly along Elbow Drive, prolonging the trolley-versus-bus debate. Transit driver Ted Kendricks remembered the electric wagons as "the most wonderful thing in the world," much "smoother and quieter" than the old streetcars. Trolley coaches played a vital role in Calgary's postwar rush to modernization. "Half a step after the introduction of the trolley onto city streets as the modern thing," wrote reporter Frank Dabbs, "Calgary waltzed into its salad days of growth and expansion." By 1957, "the heyday of the trolley," there were 105 coaches, no street cars and only 60 gas-powered buses.[8]

Yet Kendricks admitted feeling "freer in a diesel," pointing out the disadvantages of wired buses. "You'd go through the switches and you'd cross your fingers." Those ugly overhead wires meant fixed routes, making emergency re-routing difficult and express "leap-frogging" service impossible. Finally, new electric coaches were now double the capital cost of their diesel brothers. While chief engineer Wray endorsed the continued use of trolley coaches on heavily travelled traditional routes, he advocated that new additions to the Calgary Transit fleet be buses. Diesel buses were needed to "most efficiently operate" light routes, permit extension of service to newly developed areas, operate express routes and provide charter service.[9]

Express bus service had already begun. In October 1957, Green, Red and Yellow Pennant Express buses started rush-hour service between downtown and Wildwood, Killarney and Capitol Hill. Then in February 1969, all-day Blue Arrow Express service began to Varsity Acres in the northwest and Manchester in the south, pioneering traffic corridors for the first two stages of Calgary's future light-rail-transit system. Four years later, the old trolley coaches began disappearing from city streets, after council decided to convert entirely to diesels for economic reasons. Coach 445's last run on the Elbow Drive route on Saturday, March 12,

South Calgary bus, 1956. (Glenbow Archives NA–2864–1966)

1975, marked the end of the line for Calgary's postwar fleet of electric transit vehicles.

The Automobile Triumphant

Trolley coaches or diesel buses? It mattered little as public transit lost out to the private automobile in postwar Calgary. While the city's population almost doubled between 1946 and 1956, ridership on public transit actually fell from 27.0 million to 26.8 million annual passengers. Old routes were extended and new routes added to keep pace with Calgary's ever-stretching boundaries, yet the decline continued. By 1961, due in part to a 43-day strike by transit operators, ridership dipped below the 20 million mark for the first time since before the Second World

War. As patronage fell, annual operating deficits spiralled upward. As fares were increased to cover cash shortfalls, patrons continued to desert public transit.

Social commentators might attribute declining bus ridership to a reduced work week (from six to five days for most postwar Calgarians), or to stay-at-home evenings as television triumphed over movies. Yet the real villain was the family car. Automobile registrations in Calgary tripled from 13,500 in 1947 to 42,000 in 1957, then more than doubled again to over 100,000 five years later. By 1962, reported the *Herald*, Calgary Transit "has lost one out of every three passengers in its tussle with the auto."[10]

The Alberta Motor Association's December 1963 move into its new Calgary office at 8th Street and 11th Avenue SW symbolized the triumph of the automobile. Here in a modernistic two-storey building, costing $325,000 and housing communications, driver training, emergency, insurance and travel

Esso station, 4th Street SW, 1955. (Glenbow Archives NA–5093–79)

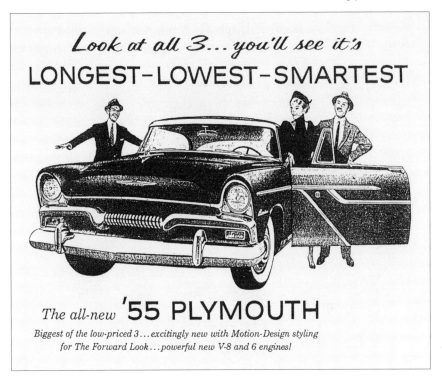

Look at all 3... you'll see it's

LONGEST-LOWEST-SMARTEST

The all-new '55 PLYMOUTH

*Biggest of the low-priced 3... excitingly new with Motion-Design styling
for The Forward Look... powerful new V-8 and 6 engines!*

1957 Plymouth advertisement. *(The Calgary Herald)*

services, the AMA served some 58,000 members. "Calgary today has more motor vehicles per capita than any other city on the continent except Los Angeles," proudly reported the *Herald*.[11]

Reporter Dave Green captured the increasing domination of the automobile in a March 1957 *Herald* article:

Every day, from every corner of this big, sprawling city, over bridges, cloverleafs, arterial thoroughfares, from side streets and country highways, hundreds of cars pour into the downtown district. The first wave to hit the city are the workers, who arrive at 8:00 AM. At 9:00 AM, the executives appear, and throughout the day shoppers come and go in a ceaseless stream. One wonders where all the automobiles can be put up, and watching the evening exodus, one marvels at where they all came from.[12]

And they kept coming. Seven years later, a city study showed that 72 percent of downtown-bound travellers came by automobile and only 28 percent by public transit.[13] Green's article had been headlined, "Downtown Calgary Wants the People; But It's a Question of Where to Put All the Cars." Calgary's first parking meters were installed along 7th, 8th and 9th avenues,

"Not yet, son. Wait till it gets real bad." 1953. (The Calgary Herald)

DPC Parkade, 9th Avenue and Centre Street, 1955. (City of Calgary Archives PP-00503)

between 2nd Street SE and 4th Street SW, in September 1948. Rates were 12 minutes for one cent, up to a maximum of an hour for five cents, between 9 a.m. and 6 p.m., Monday through Saturday. While meters offered a short-term parking solution for shoppers, they did little to ease the strain on day-long workers who wanted to bring their cars downtown in 1948. Few employers offered their own private parking lots, while two city-run metered lots offered only five-hour maximums.

Parking had improved markedly by the time of Green's 1957 article. Calgary's Downtown Parking Corporation operated seven lots totalling 500 stalls, handling 50,000 cars a month. Add to this the Hudson's Bay Company's five-storey, 650-stall parking garage (2,000 cars per day) and the T. Eaton Company's six-deck, 375-stall garage (another 1,500 cars), plus several privately owned lots offering more than 900 additional spaces. Five years later, in November 1962, Mayor Harry Hays snipped the red ribbon to open the largest downtown parking structure of its kind in Canada. The $2,000,000 addition to the Bay Parkade provided 640 more stalls, entrances from both 6th and 7th Avenue SW, and direct access to the store's pedestrian "skywalk" over 7th Avenue. It "will help keep the downtown alive," said Hays. "Without a real live downtown a city does not have the character it should have."[14]

Yet parking depended on getting downtown in the first place. Motorists from the south fumed when CPR trains halted traffic at the 4th Street SW level crossing. By September 1950, this rail crossing saw 1300 cars an hour, 2000 at peak times. That month, city council approved an $800,000 subway to carry 4th Street under both the CPR tracks and 9th Avenue, with cloverleaf connections to 9th Avenue. "It would be nice to think that this was the first installment of an orderly plan to improve the layout of Calgary," mused the *Herald*.[15] Two years later, in June 1952, North Hill shoppers and commuters, forced to cross the Bow River, found partial relief when traffic lights at the south end of Louise Bridge (9th Street and 4th Avenue) increased flow by more than 650 vehicles an hour.

Traffic synchronization was another piece of the puzzle. "With thousands of cars and trucks and all kinds of big buses cruising our streets," charged the *Herald* in June 1951, "the haphazard placing of traffic lights and their imperfect synchronization, the inadequacy of traffic signs and the failure to plan a through-street system, can no longer be tolerated." Modernization demanded that the traffic department hurry up with its "surveying and planning for traffic light synchronization and a through-street system ... for only by attacking these basic problems will traffic in Calgary be speeded up and properly controlled."[16]

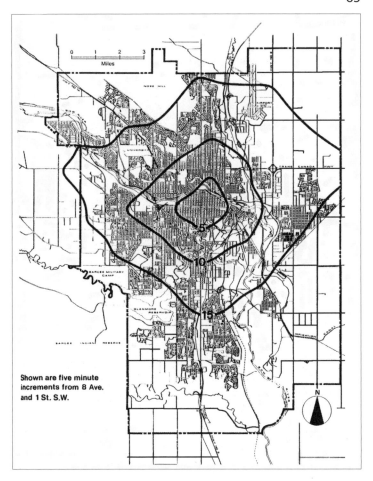

Auto travel time, 1964. (Baine. *Calgary: An Urban Study.* 1973.)

In November 1954, city traffic engineer W.D. Grant outlined three possibilities for speeding up traffic flow into and through the downtown core:

Traffic in downtown Calgary has reached the point where, under present arrangements, the streets have reached their point of maximum flow. To relieve this condition, the rate

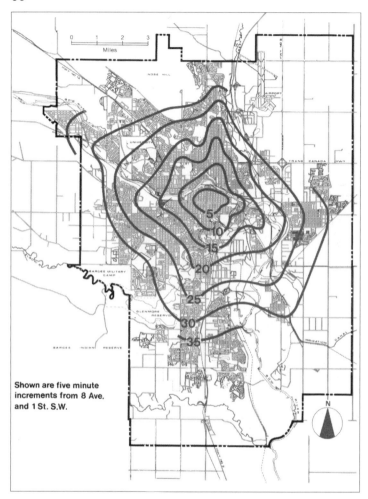

Shown are five minute
increments from 8 Ave.
and 1 St. S.W.

Transit travel time, 1964. (Baine. *Calgary: An Urban Study*. 1973.)

of traffic movement must be increased by one or more of
three methods: by removal of parking in the most congested
areas, by purchase of property and widening of streets, or
by the use of one-way streets. The first method ... has an
effect on land and business values and should not be used

unless other methods are unavailable or inadequate. The second ... is extremely expensive ... making such procedure impractical. The third ... is relatively inexpensive and has little, if any, adverse effect on land and business values.[17]

One-way traffic was subsequently introduced to downtown Calgary: westbound on 6th Avenue, eastbound on 9th; northbound on 2nd Street, southbound on 3rd. "The actual effect of one-way streets on traffic is most beneficial," Grant predicted. "Volumes are increased between 50 and 100 percent, speeds of traffic increased, and points of accident conflict at intersections decreased." Business, too, would benefit in Grant's streamlined, modern world. "Mass transportation schedules and headway improve through decreased interference making this means of transportation more appealing to more people. Economic savings in time, gasoline, and accident repairs are effected to motorists and commercial transport firms. Merchants benefit through greater accessibility, increased safety, and fewer delays for patrons."[18]

Still, the downtown Calgary situation continued critical. "The extraordinary growth of the city since the end of the Second Great War," pronounced the *Herald* in March 1957, "has threatened the downtown area with a kind of dry-rot." Suburban shopping centres, handling less traffic than city centre, were attracting customers away from downtown. "Such a trend can threaten the existence of the city itself," the *Herald* predicted, "for with the nucleus removed, the residents of different districts will have no common meeting ground, and district pride will replace the old conception of civic pride."[19]

Linking and Bridging

This steady and spectacular increase in automobiles brought pressure for continued improvements to the city's transportation infrastructure. While one-way streets and parking buildings were created to ease the flow of subdivision dwellers into the downtown, new arterial roads and trails were built as automobile commuter routes lengthened into the furthest, newest subdivisions.

Beyond the downtown core, city engineers and traffic

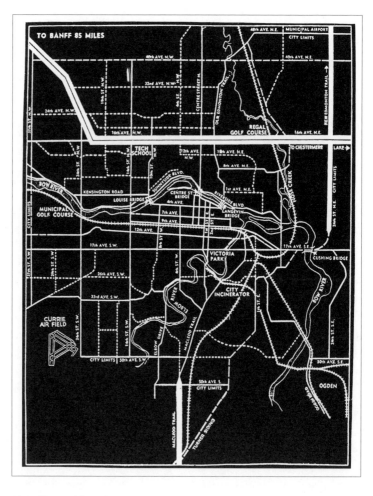

Major thoroughfare plan, 1952. *(The Calgary Herald)*

experts addressed problems of moving vehicles more economically and efficiently around Calgary. The Major Thoroughfare Plan of 1954 designated four categories of major streets: (1) arterial thoroughfares, including provincial highways and main connections between them, 132-foot (40 metre) widths; (2) major thoroughfares, those main streets serving as connections between one part of the city and another, 100-foot (30-metre) widths; (3) secondary thoroughfares, streets connecting with major thoroughfares and serving as collectors for residential neighbourhoods and industrial areas, 80-foot (24-metre) widths; and (4) parkways, streets established through scenic parts of the city, varying widths.[20] Nine years later, the 1963 General Plan spoke of local streets, primary collectors, arterials, high-standard express routes and parkways.

Planners identified Northmount, Fairmount and Elbow

Drawing of Glenmore & Macleod intersection. (Glenbow Archives NA-2864-1936-5)

drives as collector streets, with local commercial zones offering convenient service outlets at major intersections. Yet as geographer Donald Harasym has written:

> Each of these routes forms a continuous system passing through many neighbourhoods, and thus, to a larger extent negates one of the basic principles of residential planning, the elimination of through traffic from residential areas. These collectors, functioning as arterial roadways, split the neighbourhoods rather than bound them, and undermine the physical unity that neighbourhood units are normally expected to have. The routes have also encouraged the development of commercial pockets which cause traffic congestion and reduce safety, particularly for children whose schools are often located along the same collector streets.[21]

The Bow River presented the major barrier to efficient north-south traffic flows. For many long years after construction of the Centre Street Bridge (1916), and a new Louise Bridge (1921), the Bow's western stretch remained unspanned for miles until the Shouldice Bridge linked Montgomery and Bowness beyond the city limits. "We Need Another Bridge Across the Bow," read a 1947 newspaper headline, with the *Herald* editorial calling for a crossing between the Centre Street and Louise bridges to serve the Sunnyside neighbourhood.[22] With all due respect to Sunnyside, however, population growth was much greater in newer communities to the west and northwest.

Alderman George Brown was the first civic official to publicly champion a bridge at 14th Street. As chair of Calgary's town planning commission, he foresaw the inevitability of a link between the West Hillhurst and Sunalta districts. "Some day it will come," Brown told a January 1949 meeting of the Calgary Real Estate Board. Work on the new Mewata Bridge began in July 1953, when Mayor Don Mackay wielded a pneumatic drill and broke the pavement at 14th Street and 9th Avenue SW, describing the future bridge as the "most outstanding step ever taken to change the pattern of traffic in the building of a new community."[23]

Designed by consulting engineers Haddin, Davis & Brown of Calgary, and built by Baynes, Manning Limited of Vancouver, the Mewata Bridge carried five traffic lanes, each 3.5 metres wide, three of which were initially earmarked for rush-hour traffic. Two innovative construction aspects characterized the new structure: its 63-metre centre section was North America's longest box-girder span, while the new technique of butt-welding the reinforcing steel was used for the first time in Canada.

Mewata was more than just a bridge. "Equal consideration should be given to the aesthetic features," urged its engineers. They called for exploiting "the natural beauty inherent in a structure carefully proportioned." Such a project could be an asset to a community. "This is particularly true of this area which is potential parkland, especially on the north side of the river where much has already been achieved to this end."[24]

Haddin, Davis & Brown also proposed an elaborate system of cloverleaf interchanges, grade separations and one-way streets to ease traffic flowing on and off the span. The bridge's northern approach carried 14th Street over Westmount Boulevard (later renamed Memorial Drive), with a ramp and partial cloverleaf facilitating traffic to and from the northwest. South of the river, engineers advocated twin cloverleaf and grade-separated interchanges. Downtown-bound traffic would flow off the bridge directly onto 7th Avenue SW, which would become one-way eastbound. At the same time, one-way westbound 9th Avenue SW would allow traffic to enter the bridge without stopping.

After considerable bickering, second thoughts and motions re-opened for debate, city council finally settled on westbound 6th Avenue and eastbound 9th Avenue as one-way streets.

Motorists caught on quickly to the new traffic pattern, city police said, considering the "radical change required in driving habits." Afternoon rush-hour motorists reported the flow of traffic from westbound 6th Avenue onto the new bridge was "fast and smooth."

The Mewata Bridge was officially opened on December 6, 1954. Despite some residual sympathy for such a prosaic name as "The 14th Street Bridge," city council designated the new span "Mewata," symbolizing links with the past. Nearby stood the venerable Mewata Armouries and Mewata Stadium, both commemorating a Cree word meaning "to be happy." Native chiefs from the Stoney, Sarcee and Blackfoot nations, sons and grandsons of men who had known the Bow River before any bridges, attended the opening ceremonies.[25]

Mewata is Calgary's best example of postwar, modernistic bridge design. Higher above water level than the older Louise Bridge to the east, Mewata emphasizes a streamlined horizontality missing in the later Crowchild Bridge to the west. "Modernistic in design," enthused the *Financial Post*, a "milestone in the city's vast postwar development."[26] Remembering their native predecessors, and gunning their new-model cars, Calgary motorists could be both happy and modern on the new Mewata Bridge.

Crowchild was next. Continued subdivision development in the northwest and southwest, fuelled in large part by the burgeoning University of Calgary campus, strained Mewata's capacity through the early and mid-1960s. Such pressures combined to produce late modernist examples of both highway building and bridge construction. The $17,000,000 24th Street Expressway (rechristened Crowchild Trail when opened in November 1967) proved a classic example of brutal modernism as it spewed noise and pollution, endangered schools, reduced property values and disrupted neighbourhoods—all to serve the automobile and Calgary's suburban populations.

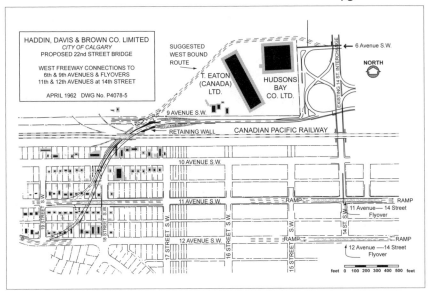

Proposed Crowchild connections, 1962. (Calgary City Archives, Map 000069)

The Crowchild Bridge over the Bow River, with final costs more than doubling the original $6,500,000 estimate, connected the north and south corridors of the new expressway. With its complicated interchanges on both sides of the river resulting in frequent lane-changing, the bridge certainly posed a challenge for many city motorists. Even before it opened, the bridge was assailed by critics for both engineering and aesthetic deficiencies. Alderman Dave Russell branded it as "ugly" and called on the city to "take steps to improve the aesthetics of future developments on the complex and expressway."[27] Yet though the Crowchild lacked the majesty of Centre Street Bridge, the quaintness of Louise Bridge and the streamlined simplicity of Mewata, it succeeded in its primary goal—speeding automobile traffic around and through the city.

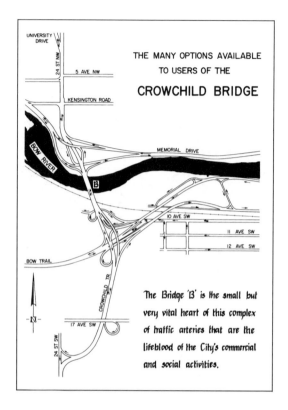

THE MANY OPTIONS AVAILABLE TO USERS OF THE

CROWCHILD BRIDGE

The Bridge 'B' is the small but very vital heart of this complex of traffic arteries that are the lifeblood of the City's commercial and social activities.

Options for Crowchild Bridge. (Welin, *The Bridges of Calgary, 1882-1977.* City of Calgary. 1977)

Highways and Flyways

Both the Mewata and Crowchild bridges were seen as links, not just between Calgary neighbourhoods split by the Bow River, but also with existing and proposed highway developments north and south of the city. Highways minister Gordon Taylor represented the province (and Alberta's $700,000 contribution) at Mewata's opening in December 1954. He welcomed the bridge as a vital arterial link between the Banff highway to the north and future provincial highways to the south. At the opening of the Crowchild Bridge 13 years later, the Banff highway had solidified as the Trans-Canada and "future provincial highways to the south" had taken concrete shape as the Glenmore bypass and an improved Macleod Trail.

The Trans-Canada's route through or around Calgary proved a topic of intense speculation during the early postwar years. The old eastern approach (now Highway 1A connecting Inglewood and Forest Lawn and along 17th Avenue SE to Chestermere Lake) was hampered by two narrow bridges, the Cushing Bridge over the Bow River, and a second structure over an irrigation canal. This bottleneck suggested that a better route would lay in a northern by-pass, well north of McCall Field. By April 1950, however, city officials were correctly "under the impression" that the four-lane highway "will come in on 16 Avenue NE from the Forest Lawn and Albert Park direction."[28]

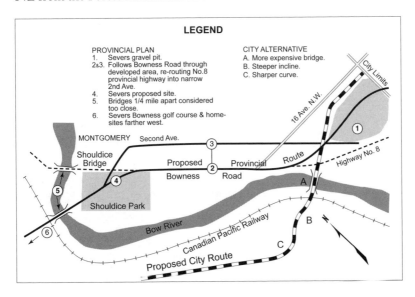

Proposed Trans-Canada Highway routes, 1954. *(The Calgary Herald)*

Canada's newest and finest MOTOR HOTEL...

★

Crossroads . . . the <u>million</u> dollar concept of travel accommodation . . . is nearing completion in Calgary. Crossroads will open in February with 65 luxury bed-sitting rooms and suites — each with shower bath, complimentary TV and phone. Just minutes away from airport and business centre, Crossroads will be a focal point for both business and social life. With all the amenities—including commanding view of the Rockies—Crossroads' rates will be pleasantly sensible. Plan to stop with us!

Featuring:

The Safari Room
for dining, receptions, banquets

Suites for families or conferences

Coffee shop, beverage room

Maid and valet service

Swimming pool in season

PARKING SPACE ADJOINING ROOMS
– AND FOR 300 EXTRA CARS

CROSSROADS

JUNCTION OF TRANS-CANADA AND #2 HIGHWAYS
CALGARY, ALBERTA

Advertisement, 1956. (*Financial Post*)

In northwest Calgary, the old Banff Highway angled north from 16th Avenue NW along Banff Trail and via today's Crowchild Trail to Cochrane and beyond. Initially, the city hoped "to preserve the splendid view of the Bow Valley" by banning all "signs, billboards and advertising devices" on the southwest side of Banff Trail.[29] But Motel Village and McMahon Stadium eventually blocked out those views, while the Trans-Canada forsook the Crowchild Trail exit for a more southern route. Highways minister Taylor announced in July 1954 that the national highway would follow an extension of 16th Avenue through Montgomery and Bowness and westward on the south side of the Bow River.

Meanwhile at McCall Field in northeast Calgary, north of the new Trans-Canada Highway, Trans-Canada Airlines began east-west flights through Calgary on July 2, 1946, using 14-passenger Lockheed Lodestars. By February 1947, TCA upgraded to 21-passenger DC3 aircraft, and by June 1948 to 40-passenger DC4 North Stars, with two flights daily to Vancouver (2 hours, 40 minutes), Winnipeg, Toronto (7 hours, 50 minutes) and Montreal. "Combining speed with operating efficiency and comfort," proclaimed TCA's advertising, the North Star sky liners were the "most advanced air liners plying the skies of this country." They offered "cabin comfort at any altitude," with large luxurious chairs spaced to give ample leg room and leave everyone room to move around. Reduced flying time, complimentary hot meals and attentive steward and stewardess service, all added "to the delight of your trip, at no extra cost."[30]

In the early 1950s, with ever-increasing TCA and Canadian Pacific Air Lines flights, and with the route of the Trans-Canada Highway determined, airport officials turned their attention to the need for a more modern terminal building if Calgary were to keep pace with other western cities of its size. In 1951, the city began planning for a new passenger terminal on the west side of the

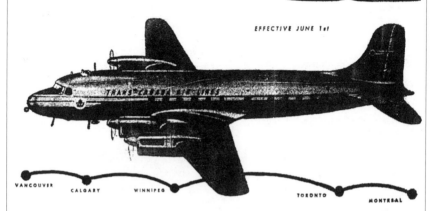

North Star Sky Liners advertisement, 1948. *(The Calgary Herald)*

field, approved a bylaw to provide necessary money, and engaged architects Ken Bond and Jack Clayton to begin design work. Five years later the new building opened as the most modern airport terminal in Canada at that time.

The basic principle used as a yardstick in planning the new terminal, reported *Canadian Aviation* magazine in a preview article, was "flexibility both in concept and execution." Public utility and convenience for the air traveller at the most reasonable cost were regarded as fundamental requirements. The design was simple and based upon a clear-cut structural framing layout. The structure "lends itself to the use of new materials and much glass and native stone for aesthetic effect is in evidence," continued the article. "Materials are being chosen for their low-maintenance upkeep, for easy erectibility, removal and replacement, and are

Passenger arrivals, 1966. (Glenbow Archives NA–2864–494d)

PWA's inaugural Air Bus, 1963. (Glenbow Archives NA–2864–4228)

generally light in character to express the characteristics of our modern air age."[31]

Yet the new terminal could barely cope with ever-increasing numbers of flights and passengers. By 1960, American carriers Western Airlines and Air West (later Hughes Air West) operated out of Calgary. TCA began jet service into the city in January 1961, with transcontinental service to Montreal, Toronto and Vancouver. Next year, Canadian Pacific inaugurated non-stop flights between Calgary and Amsterdam, Pacific Western Airlines began its "Airbus" service to Edmonton in 1963, and Time Air followed with flights to Lethbridge and Medicine Hat.

Despite additions to Canada's "most modern air terminal," a new structure eventually would have to be built. In the three-year period between 1962–1965, landings and takeoffs increased by 23 percent, passengers by 37 percent.[32] In April 1967, as the modern age wound down, city council returned the airport to Transport Canada for $2,000,000 plus a commitment from the federal government to build a new terminal.

Machines for Traffic

Yet the automobile, more than the aeroplane, brought modern transportation home to Calgarians in the 1950s and 1960s. The perspective of the new man in the new car generated the paradigms of 20th-century modernist urban planning and design. The new man, Le Corbusier said, needed "a new type of street," that would be "a machine for traffic," or "a factory for producing traffic." A truly modern street must therefore be "as well equipped as a factory." In this street, as in the modern factory, argues Marshall Berman, the best-equipped model is the thoroughly automated: "no people, except for people operating machines; no unarmored and unmechanized pedestrians to slow the flow," with the macadam belonging "to traffic alone."[33]

This form of modernism left deep marks on the lives of all Calgary residents. City development during the postwar decades "systematically attacked, and often successfully obliterated, the moving chaos of nineteenth-century urban life." The old street, with its volatile mixture of people and traffic, businesses and homes, rich and poor, was "sorted out and split up into separate compartments" in the new urban environment, continues Berman, with entrances and exits strictly monitored and controlled, loading

82

and unloading behind the scenes, parking lots and underground garages the only mediation.[34]

Modern Calgary juxtaposed vertical structures with horizontal lines, featuring vehicular flow as well as architectural form. Transportation developments helped the city experience rapid and dynamic growth, as it added new subdivisions and annexed neighbouring communities at a dizzying pace. Thanks to the automobile, by the mid-1960s Calgary would become a city without suburbs—a quintessentially modern, seamless city with a single municipal authority to control and streamline its approach to subdivision development, and a unified transportation policy to nurture and sustain that growth.

chapter 4

The Postwar Dream House

Building the Bungalows

Postwar Calgarian with new house and new car. (Glenbow Archives NC–60–20)

One hundred and fifty Calgary families began the modern era in the autumn of 1947 when they moved into their new homes in the area between 4th and 8th Streets and 24th and 26th Avenues in the North Mount Pleasant district of the city. With down payments ranging from $1,570 to $2,260, these new homeowners took possession of four-room bungalows, priced between $6,450 and $6,800, or six-room, storey-and-a-half houses from $6,900 to $7,700, on lots averaging 50 by 120 feet (15 by 37 metres). Living rooms featured fireplaces with electric or gas heaters, bedrooms boasted large closets and full-sized basements were "adaptable for a large rumpus room or easily converted into an extra room." Exteriors were graced by concrete front steps, ornamental handrails and sidewalks at front and rear. Homeowners were responsible for their own landscaping, with "top soil on the property ready for spreading."[1]

These 150 new dwellings in North Mount Pleasant came none too soon. As early as January 1945, in a speech to the newly formed Calgary Builders' Exchange, City Commissioner V.A. Newhall predicted "tremendous house building activity" in the city following the end of the Second World War.[2] Even without the immediate crush of veterans and the forthcoming demands of the expanding petroleum industry, postwar Calgary desperately needed new and improved housing. The 1941 Canadian census recorded some 8,300 "sub-standard" dwellings in the city—houses needing external repair and houses lacking or with shared use of flush toilets and bathing facilities. That figure represented 38 percent of all Calgary dwellings, not bad when compared to Edmonton's 46 percent, but shocking compared with 36 percent for Winnipeg and just 27 percent for Vancouver.[3]

"Families are anxiously looking for better places in which to live," argued Humphrey Carver in his 1948 book, *Houses for Canadians*. After years of Depression and war, "hungry for an interval of peace and stability, the people start again to build the houses that they must have for the raising of a new generation." Good, new housing must drive old, sub-standard housing "out of circulation" because a "direct relationship exists between health and the physical conditions under which people live." A family would be healthier and happier living in a house of its own that "is easy to keep clean, can be maintained at a desirable temperature, provides some privacy for each individual and a generally stimulating atmosphere of light and colour." The full benefits of improved housing, concluded Carver, would influence "the child population and the real extent of these benefits could only be properly measured over a lifetime."[4]

By 1947, the average cost of building such basic houses as Calgary's North Mount Pleasant bungalows and storey-and-a-halfs increased 80 percent over pre-war figures. Shortages and higher costs of building materials contributed to increased prices. Yet buyers themselves steadily increased their expectations. Amenities typical only of luxury bungalows of the late 1930s had by the late 1940s become commonplace, as postwar bungalows were fully insulated, with built-in kitchen cabinets and inlaid linoleum on kitchen and bathroom floors. In 1947, the average cost of these basic houses reached $6,374.[5]

While increased amenities meant higher prices, there was no stopping residential building in postwar Calgary. August 1948 witnessed a fourfold increase in construction over the previous year, and the value of building permits issued by the city passed

Calgary Home Builders Assn. Basic Cost Estimates for 1947			
building incidentals	$185	painting, glazing	335
excavation	138	roofing, sheet metal	65
concrete work	429	plumbing	575
masonry work	105	heating	250
carpentry	3,065	electrical fixtures	180
lath, plaster, stucco	872	grading, sidewalks	83
tile work	18		
finishing hardware	74	Total (excluding land)	$6,374

the $1,000,000 mark. By 1949, Calgary enjoyed the greatest construction boom in its history to date. Building permits totalled $21.8 million, topping the previous record year of 1912. Housing starts zoomed to 1,893, a 25 percent increase over the 1946 record. Almost 6,000 new homes were constructed in the city in the four years following the end of the war.[6]

In November 1955, the Calgary House Builders Association (CHBA), representing a majority of the construction, supply and sub-contracting firms in the single-family dwelling industry, submitted an impressive report to the federal Royal Commission on Canada's Economic Prospects:

Year	No. of Houses	Average Cost	Total Value
1950	2074	$9,125	$18,805,462
1951	1304	11.376	14,834,700
1952	2131	12,002	25,576,397
1953	2015	12,399	24,984,911
1954	2041	12,153	24,803,586
1955	2564	12,007	30,784,745

That came to a six-year total of 12,129 houses for a combined value of $140 million; over the 1956–60 period, the CHBA predicted another 15,600 homes, at an average cost of $11,500, for a total of $180 million.

Hopefully, costs could be held in line. Yet by the mid-1950s, the city required house builders in new project areas to provide all local improvements—including water mains and sewers, curbs and gutters, sidewalks and gravelled roads—resulting in builders passing along an average additional cost of $1,100 per house. The CHBA expressed concern about financing housing for average wage earners. By the mid-1950s, some 80 percent of

Better Homes Exposition advertisement, 1949. *(The Calgary Herald)*

the local building industry was financed through mortgage money advanced to lending institutions under the National Housing Act. The $11,500 average cost of a single-family dwelling called for a $1,900 down payment and a $9,600 mortgage. This made it "practically impossible for the average wage earner in Calgary to purchase a house," for at wages of $60 per week or $3,100 per year, this wage earner could obtain a maximum mortgage of only $7,500.

Calgary's early postwar house-building industry was characterized by small contractors who erected few units per year—seven different contractors, for example, built North Mount Pleasant's 150 new dwellings during 1947. George Olson typified the successful Calgary builder. After bouncing around as a

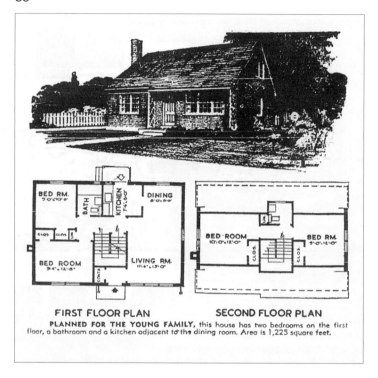

FIRST FLOOR PLAN   SECOND FLOOR PLAN

PLANNED FOR THE YOUNG FAMILY, this house has two bedrooms on the first floor, a bathroom and a kitchen adjacent to the dining room. Area is 1,225 square feet.

Floor plan for 1949 house. *(The Calgary Herald)*

farm labourer, builder of grain elevators, butcher and RCAF cook, 30-year-old George went into partnership with his brother Vic as Olson Bros. Construction began immediately after the war. They acquired seven lots on 20th Avenue NE, east of Edmonton Trail, at $150 apiece, built houses on them and sold each at a profit. George later established his own up-scale firm, George Olson Custom Built Homes, later formed Plateau Land Development with two partners and eventually developed Westgate and Southwood communities.[7]

Ellis Keith was even more successful. After trying office work, photography and running an egg-grading station, 26-year-

Laying water main, 1949. (Glenbow Archives NA–2597–69)

old Keith built a four-room house in 1944 as a hobby, sold it for $5,200, and used the proceeds to launch his contracting career. He then built 46 houses in Montgomery, just beyond the city limits, selling them for $2,500 apiece. "Rabbit-hutch houses," he called

Sidewalk construction, 1958. (Glenbow Archives NA–5093–480)

them. "They didn't win any design awards but they filled a need." When Montgomery ran out of available land, Keith built 130 homes in Parkdale. As vacant lots in built-up areas grew scarce, he moved into large-scale land acquisition in southwest Calgary.

Through the 1950s and into the '60s, the Keith name was prominent in subdivision expansion and home building in Glendale, Highwood, Wildwood, Kingsland and Haysboro. By the time he moved into Willow Park and Lake Bonavista during the mid-1960s, Keith had come a long way from the rabbit-hutch projects of his early career. Willow Park received a golf course, Lake Bonavista an artificial lake, and all Keith neighbourhoods were endowed with grass, parks, community centres, playgrounds, skating rinks, tot-lots and mature trees.[8]

A pronounced trend toward larger residential builders, encouraged by the CMHC, emerged during the 1950s. Like Keith Construction, these firms developed and planned entire residential areas, handling all aspects of residential construction from land acquisition through servicing, house construction and sales. One of the boldest was Nu-West, which soon became the largest home builder in the city. Nu-West's success rested partly on its ability to control land. Incorporated as Nu-West Homes Limited in 1946, the company took off in 1957 when 28-year-old Ralph Scurfield, a former teacher and construction worker, bought a one-quarter share with $15,000, moved from Edmonton to Calgary and took over as president.

Scurfield began by inspecting and repairing homes built by Nu-West's former owners and introducing a five-year warranty, the first in Canada. Nu-West built 65 homes in 1957—15 more than the previous year—and turned a handsome profit. The following year, Nu-West became a founding member of Carma Developers Ltd., a mega-company formed to acquire and assemble land. During the 1970s, Nu-West became the major shareholder as Carma expanded into commercial real estate, and into the

Stampede Dream Home, 1958. (Glenbow Archives NA–5093–449)

Edmonton and American markets. By 1981 Carma produced almost 30 percent of the serviced residential lots in Calgary, and one-fifth of the city's population lived in Carma-developed communities.[9]

From Bungalows to Split-Levels

The prototypical 1950s Calgary bungalow debuted in October 1949 as the model home in the Calgary Better Homes Exposition at the Stampede grounds. Built by the Calgary House Builders' Association, this four-room $8,100 bungalow reflected both an increase in housing prices and a pronounced trend toward flatter, lower dwellings. Attractively (if somewhat blandly) finished in horizontal bands of white clapboard siding and stucco, the exterior featured a small porch flanked with wrought-iron work, with glass bricks set on either side of the entrance door "for both decorative and light-giving qualities." Inside, the living-dining room featured the latest in modern home design—a "large picture window and a wall of bleached-birch plywood."[10]

The bungalow soon dominated Calgary residential architecture. While New York boasts the loft as its most pervasive residential unit, claims Calgary architecture professor John Brown, "we have bungalows—blocks and blocks and blocks of bungalows."[11] By 1958, eight out of 10 houses built in Calgary were single-storey bungalows with hip or gabled roofs. Within a few years, the average bungalow grew from a floor space of some 900 square feet (84 square metres) to around 1,200 square feet (112 square metres), reflecting both their appeal and the growing affluence of the city's inhabitants. The bungalow's strong horizontal lines spoke to the modernist outlook of postwar couples. At the same time, they were remarkably well suited to the prairie landscape, where trees are low and these buildings can be more easily sheltered than the high rise structure of earlier years.[12]

Stampede Dream Home, 1960. (Glenbow Archives NA–5093–799)

The ideal of the horizontal house, which a *Better Homes and Gardens* survey showed was well established across the United States by 1950, had originally been worked out in the American Midwest by Frank Lloyd Wright and the Prairie School of architecture. But most people associated it with California, where a well-established modernist tradition had merged Wright's ideas with those coming out of Europe during the 1920s and adapted both to the mild Pacific climate.[13] By the early 1950s, a very basic, stripped-down version of this Wrightian/Californian horizontal bungalow arrived in Calgary. Now, the typical new house in a newly developed Calgary subdivision was long and low, with horizontal bands of clapboard (or later, aluminum siding) and stucco, often in different, high-contrast colours.

Stronger and more pronounced horizontal house lines prompted changes in landscape design. Front lawns emphasized plantings that stressed horizontal rather than vertical elements. "Don't make the mistake of planting tall growing trees or shrubs close to the house, where they will bar the view from windows and keep the interior in steady shade," the *Herald* advised its readers in June 1945. "Let these, if used at all for foundation planting, be located at corners, with smaller and low-growing plants beneath the windows and by the steps." Groundcovers and low trees and shrubs, reinforcing the horizontal line of the house without blocking the view of the yard from the large window, were to be used. Shrubbery and flower beds should occupy only the sides of rear lawns, with shrubbery again at the back.[14]

Combine this emphasis on horizontal plantings with the treeless nature of most new Calgary building lots, factor in the financial realities that confronted most new homeowners, and the result was street after street of houses unrelieved by any vertical greenery. "They are not landscaping but scalping," charged Alderman Mary Dover. "These new sites are being flattened too much."[15] In time, however, the large picture windows that increasingly characterized postwar living rooms and even kitchens led to attempts to make lawns and gardens private and to prevent passersby from seeing into houses, especially from back alleys. This put an increased emphasis on fences and trees around the perimeter of the lot, with fences becoming higher and higher, especially when a demand for patios developed in the 1960s.[16]

Increasingly through the 1960s, the term "ranch style" was applied to many Calgary bungalows, generally referring to larger, more luxurious examples on larger lots in pricier neighbourhoods. These ranch styles emphasized even stronger horizontal lines, with overhanging eaves and hip or gable roofs. Most continued to be rectangular in design, sited parallel to the street across the front of the property, although L-shapes were also popular.

The split-level house also emerged in Calgary in the 1950s and 1960s. Split-levels put part of the living space—perhaps a rumpus room or guest bedroom, along with a half-bath and laundry room—into what would otherwise be a basement. Half a level above that was the front door of the house, along with living room, dining room and kitchen. Family bedrooms were another half level above. The split-level seemed more convenient than an ordinary two-storey house—because of the ease of walking up six or seven steps rather than a whole flight of stairs—while still providing a desirable separation between living and sleeping areas. In addition, builders were able to pass along construction savings and offer more house for the money.[17]

Calgary became one of the nation's leaders in single-family housing in the postwar period. Between 1956 and 1965, some 26,800 residential lots were developed. Kelwood Corporation led the way with 9,296 lots (35 percent of the total), and was most active in the Acadia, Chinook Park, Eagle Ridge, Fairview, Glendale, Haysboro, Highwood, Kingsland, Mayfair and Wildwood districts. Nu-West/Carma developed another 4,525 lots (17 percent), and became dominant in the 1960s, as the new University of Calgary campus boosted development in the northwest. Carma was most active in Charleswood, Foothill Estates, Greenview, Mayland Heights, Rosemont, Southwood, University Heights and Varsity Acres.[18]

Homes for the Avant-Garde

In a feature article entitled "Decade Houses" for the September 1980 issue of *Calgary Magazine*, architecture writer Stephanie White spotlighted three modernist residences. For the 1940s, modernism's first decade in the city, she chose a small residence (since demolished) at 626 Riverdale Avenue SW:

> The front elevation is one of the clearest examples of Bauhaus-influenced design in Calgary. It sits like a three-dimensional abstract painting in black and white, with the venetian blind in the stairwell always pulled down and formal arrangement of hedge and three shrubs placed with implacable deliberateness across the front. Severe as it

appears, the house has a capacity for real richness: the front doors ... have very elegant brass hardware, the glass block panel is thick and shimmers like water—a magical thing to have in a plain stucco wall ... The building is a cubic volume instead of a traditional image, windows are panels in a composition instead of being traditionally placed according to interior convention. There is a hard intersection of walls and roof, as opposed to the gentler lines of a pitched roof.

For her mid-modernist or 1950s gem, White moved one street south and a few blocks west to 1242 Lansdowne Avenue SW:

This is a fine example of the changing relationship between the house, the street, and the automobile ... The carport tacked itself onto either the front or side, setting up a buffer between the house and the street. In the 1950s, the family and its home were an island ... Houses started to turn in on themselves and their backyards. The barbeque on the patio became *de rigueur* and the very formal living room with a large picture window provided a further buffer between the family areas at the back of the house and the outside world at the front. The house developed, over the last twenty years, into an organization of yard to building of almost oriental calm. The landscaping obscures the bulk of the house and really emphasizes the inner-sanctum quality of the original design.

Finally, for her late-modernist masterpiece, White leapfrogged from the flats of Riverdale to the bluffs of the new Eagle Ridge subdivision and a 1968 house at 24 Eagle Ridge Place SW:

The tall, elegant entrance, here a *trompe l'oeil* arrangement of flat, illusory columns and round, real ones, protects the front door. The high hedge protects the generous front yard, living is well removed from the hurly-burly by physical distance and a beautiful, intensely formal front wall. The gleaming white enamelled woodwork against the rich red brick, the fanlight over the door, the inherent calm in the arrangement of the windows.[19]

Twenty years later, for the "Calgary Modern" exhibition at the Nickle Arts Museum, architect Jeremy Sturgess underscored the importance of Calgary's hillsides and bluffs in his choices of landmark modernist residences. Through the 1940s and 1950s, argued Sturgess, modernist homes "claimed the bluffs as prime territory," and for the first time the city embraced the mountain and downtown-skyline views so characteristic of this place, thus achieving a "distinct typology that helps to establish an identifiable regional architecture for Calgary." Within this context, Sturgess selected four houses for "their clear embrace of the tenets of Modernism, for their impact on the architectural context of their time, and for their legacy as icons of a significant era in Calgary's history."[20]

Sturgess's first choice was the Dimitri Skaken House, built in 1947 at 1131 Colborne Crescent SW, a "heroic example of the Modern Movement" located amid Mount Royal's older mansions:

The house is Calgary's best remaining example of early Modernism. Stark, flat-roofed cubic forms are simply and strategically connected to create a bold and uncompromising form on the hillside landscape. Gentle curves embrace the downtown skyline. The house is finished in white stucco, the "trademark" building material of the early Modernists, and stands today as a symbol of the power of architecture to express a new way of living.

Dimitri Skaken House. (Clyde McConnell)

Next in chronological order for Sturgess was another Mount Royal residence, the Mayer Katchen House at 800 Prospect Avenue SW, built in 1954 and designed by Clayton Bond & Mogridge:

> The low-slung house artfully embraces and enfolds the landscape such that it discreetly creates an entire indoor/outdoor living realm within the confines of the site, the structure of the house is clearly expressed through exposed beams and clerestory windows. Large open spaces are tempered by built-in walnut-veneer wall systems. Tilted roofs embrace sunlight while preserving site privacy.

Sturgess found his third example in Elboya—the Trend House at 47th Avenue and Elbow Drive SW, built in 1957 and designed by Rule, Wynn & Rule as the winner of a competition sponsored by the British Columbia plywood industry:

> The house showcased the use of plywood and mass production technology as the new paradigm for modern living. In the spirit of [California's] Case Study Houses, the Trend House was the model for a new housing type for a developing middle class, and ultimately influenced Calgary suburban house design for years to come.

Meyer Katchen House. (Clyde McConnell)

Trend House. (Clyde McConnell)

Sturgess then moved north to St. Andrew's Heights and the Kalbfleisch House at 2604 Toronto Crescent NW, designed in 1964 by architect John Hondema for a prominent site overlooking the Bow River valley:

> The house is a bold expression of a later development of Corbusian Modernism. Materiality was clearly employed to express not only function but the dynamic of function; witness the massive end walls expressive of poured concrete that support a massive, upwardly soaring wood roof, which together shelter a transparent skin of glass that embraces the view. The main living areas of the house are raised to

the second level to maximize views, and to take advantage of the curved wood-clad roof. Teak interior cabinetry, coloured glass inserts, and slate floors combine to achieve an interior in harmony with the bold envelope.[21]

For their 1995 look at modern houses across the country, Graham Livesey, Michael McMordie and Geoffrey Simmins echoed Sturgess's hillside orientation in their Calgary choice: the Roenisch Residence in Eagle Ridge, designed by Jack Long and completed in 1962:

Kalbfleisch House. (Clyde McConnell)

The house is notable for two reasons: for the large glazed atrium at its heart; and for the heavy load-bearing laminated beams that confer on it a regular structural grid ... From the entryway only a hint of the glazed atrium is visible. A pierced screen of black walnut subtly delays a full view of the interior: only gradually revealed is the full extent of the square double-height atrium, covered by a octapartite folded-plate roof rising to a high peak at the centre of the court ... The main rooms are disposed strategically around the high core of the atrium. Sliding doors provide more than a hint of Japanese architecture, an effect reinforced by a lack of decorative mouldings.[22]

Although these mansions were clearly upper-class dream houses, too expensive and perhaps too formal for most wage earners, the Calgary home-owning public was at least to some degree familiar with architectural modernism—a modernism widely publicized through world's fairs, museum exhibitions, department stores, home magazines and movies. In the years following the Second World War, the spatial aesthetics established by the modernists appeared in a watered-down, mass-produced version when new housing developments across the city and across the continent offered their consumers large picture windows or glass walls and continuous living-dining areas, imitating the principle of merging spaces found in the architectural ideal.

Moving In and Decorating

The picture window quickly became an almost obligatory feature of the postwar Calgary house. While originating as a way for developers to make their tiny postwar houses feel a little more spacious than 900 or so square feet, the picture window soon made its way into virtually every style and price of house built during the period. The picture window, states Thomas Hine, "was not only a way of looking out on one's achievement but also a way of looking in." Often, it framed a lamp and other decorative items that were purchased specifically for display there. "And it also framed family life, which was visible, although not often intelligible, through the always open draperies."[23]

Behind those picture windows and open drapes, postwar Calgary house interiors made extensive use of such new construction materials as laminated and moulded plywood, tubular metal and plastic. New technologies gave birth to Arborite kitchen counters, Formica table tops and Congoleum floors. Vinyl sofas carried the notion of modern technology over to furniture. All were miracle synthetic products that, as historian Douglas

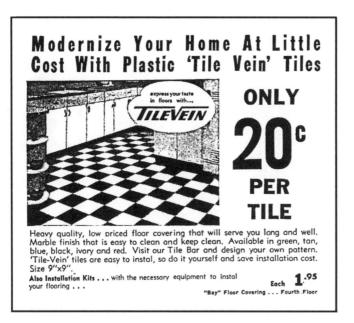

Kitchen tile advertisement. *(The Calgary Herald)*

Owram argues, "promised the cachet of the modern, and the practicality of easy maintenance and durability." Furniture design was equally self-conscious and modern. Modern easy-to-clean synthetics, butterfly chairs in the living room, moulded plywood chairs in the dining room and reclining chairs with built-in footstools provide examples of modernism in furniture design.[24]

For a significant upper-middle-class part of the market, Danish modern furniture offered the best of all possible worlds. It boasted light modern lines, carried out most often in teak, a luxurious tropical wood. Danish modern allowed its buyers to feel they were modern and respectful of the achievements of their own time and were purchasing honest, well-made furniture. This Danish look had a great impact on domestic production, too, because it inspired manufacturers to feature the wooden frame by exposing it and using loose foam cushions.

The kitchen also changed in appearance. During the late 1940s and early 1950s, with families catching up after the war, a modern kitchen was simply an old-fashioned one with many new appliances added. Each appliance was slightly streamlined; each stood on its own, a separate piece of machinery. The kitchen table often had a wooden base and an enamelled metal top, and oak chairs gave way to plastic-upholstered, tubular-metal cantilevered chairs. By the mid-1950s, however, roundness was out as a visual style, so appliances became squarer. They were also increasingly no longer seen as mere objects in the kitchen; rather, they were the kitchen, and were increasingly built into kitchens. Ovens went up on walls; burners interrupted expanses of counters; dishwashers nestled next to sinks. The environment was so clean and uninterrupted that even cupboard doors weren't allowed to have handles. Everything was recessed, hidden or built-in.[25]

Rooms began to flow together for both functional and organic reasons. Combination living-dining rooms, kitchen-

Kitchen,1958 Stampede Dream Home. (Glenbow Archives NA–5093–490)

dining areas and formal-informal living areas increasingly characterized postwar houses. Such open plans continued to be immensely popular through the 1950s and 1960s, justified on the grounds of an enhanced family life and informal lifestyles. Home magazines, manuals on interior decor and books on housing design idealized the flowing, continuous spaces of California ranch-style architecture, which followed the functionalist design principles of "easy living" by eliminating walls in the central living spaces of the home. Continuous spaces allowed residents to exert a minimum of energy by reducing the need to move from room to room.[26]

The emergence of the family room showed the "importance attached to organizing household spaces around ideals of family

Dining room,1958 Stampede Dream Home. (Glenbow Archives NA–5093–491)

togetherness."The family room began life as a playroom or rumpus room, often found in the basement of a bungalow or the lower level of a split. By the mid-1950s, it began turning into a second, more heavily used living room, and by 1960 the television set had made the move. The living room increasingly became more formal and traditional in its furnishings, while the family room had a more contemporary feel and was furnished with more durable furniture, often covered with an imitation leather marketed as Naugahyde. With its pine panelling, its brick fireplace, and comfortable sofa and chairs, the family room "exuded coziness."[27]

Once Calgary's CHIT-TV began broadcasting in late 1954, television quickly became an important family activity. Magazines typically presented the television set as the new family hearth, through which love and affection might be rekindled. Stylish television cabinets meshed with and enhanced the interior decor; new "entertainment centres," comprised of a radio, television and phonograph, often made the piano entirely obsolete. Television fit well with more general postwar hopes for a return to family values. It was seen "as a kind of household cement that promised to reassemble the splintered lives of families who had been separated

Living room,1960 Stampede Dream Home. (Glenbow Archives NA-5093-829)

TV room,1959 Stampede Dream Home. (Glenbow Archives NA–5093–679)

during the war," writes historian Lynn Spigel. It was also meant to "reinforce the new suburban family unit, which had left most of its extended family and friends behind in the city."[28]

Modernism in interior decor and furniture design suited the postwar age. Home owners, usually young married people, "had an open-minded awareness of all things modern," whether automobiles, electric refrigerators or television sets. They were interested in the future and shaped their living patterns accordingly. In addition, manufactured modern design was easily tailored to a budget-minded market. "Mass-production items, using relatively cheap materials," concludes Owram, "enabled the young family on a limited budget to have the latest in fashion cheaply."[29] Postwar interior house design was driven by a mass-market, middle-class, suburban modernism.

Refrigerator advertisement. *(The Calgary Herald)*

Automatic washer advertisement. *(The Calgary Herald)*

But Not for Everyone

Postwar economic conditions certainly encouraged home ownership. Employment rates were high, interest rates were low, wages increased steadily and living standards rose for most Canadian families. The engine driving Canada's and Alberta's housing policy after the war was the National Housing Act, administered by a new crown corporation, the Central Mortgage and Housing Corporation. In Alberta, the NHA was most important for its mortgage provisions, which permitted house mortgages at less than prevailing interest rates and with lower down payments and longer repayment periods.

Yet the NHA favoured middle and upper income groups. As in conventional loans, the amount of money an individual could borrow was tied to income, and although the ratio increased over time, in 1956 no more than 23 percent of an individual's annual income could be used for payment of principal, interest and taxes. This meant that it was difficult for anyone with an annual income less than $3,000 to qualify for an NHA mortgage. The NHA also favoured single-family detached dwellings. Government policy to 1968 assumed that by providing single detached homes for the middle class, the housing problems of those with less income would be solved through "filtering" as middle-income groups moving to the suburbs vacated smaller, older and cheaper housing for lower income groups.[30]

Despite government-backed mortgages, filtering and increased amortization periods to make houses more affordable, lower-income families were increasingly squeezed by rising housing costs. In 1955, noting that about 80 percent of new residential construction in Calgary was financed under NHA provisions, the Calgary House Builders' Association argued that it was "practically impossible" for the average wage earner ($3,100 a year) to purchase a home. The situation only worsened. By 1966, the average income of borrowers in Alberta for new homes under the NHA was about 40 percent above the national average, which meant that "average" wage earners, those earning $5,000 to $7,000 per year, were finding housing too expensive.[31]

Denied a single-family, detached house, many Calgarians turned to alternatives such as rental units and multiplexes. Most postwar duplexes and four-plexes were little different than single-family detached houses in terms of design, except that the floor plan was reversed on one side to give a central access to all the units. Through the late 1940s, low-rise, walk-up apartments began to appear in Calgary neighbourhoods, frequently imitating the pared-down designs in stucco that were common in houses of the immediate postwar years.

Spruce Cliff Apartments in southwest Calgary, overlooking the Bow River and the city skyline from Shaganappi Heights, is a series of low-rise apartment blocks designed by Rule, Wynn & Rule and built as a $7,000,000 social-housing project in 1953. Forty years later, the blocks still seem sensitively distributed across the site, establishing a park-like setting and offering remarkable views of the city. The original carports were unique because of their "butterfly" roofs. This "endorsement of the modernist aesthetic for such a significant development of public housing in Calgary," argues architect Jeremy Sturgess, illustrated a "commitment to the ideals of Modernism as the means to a healthier and enriched lifestyle."[32]

With the advent of the high rise in the mid-1950s, apartments were built deliberately to attract tenants from upper income levels. Increasingly, the more expensive high rises offered different sizes of suites and a number of different floor plans; they tended to be located in central parts of the city and were often promoted to attract tenants of similar age, family type or occupation. They provided a housing option that appealed to many people, and promotions illustrating their occupants'

Spruce Cliff Apartments advertisement. *(The Calgary Herald)*

lifestyles as glamorous helped high rises escape the reputation that had been attached to apartments through the Depression and war years. "They were seen as progressive," conclude Wetherell and Kmet, "because of their location, their aura of fashion, and their use of technologically up-to-date equipment."[33]

Rideau Towers in southwest Calgary, overlooking the Elbow River and the downtown skyline, is the city's best example of modernist, high-rise apartment construction. Built in 1963, Rideau Towers were designed by a young German-trained and Toronto-based architect, Peter Caspari. The five, seven-storey blocks of

Rideau Towers were built using a revolutionary suspended concrete slab construction technique that enabled a virtually column-free floor plan. The project remains a "remarkable exponent of this system," argues Sturgess, as the flexibility inherent in the structural system has accommodated alterations to the buildings' interiors over the years within this simple structural framework.[34] Rideau Towers represented classic modernist residential verticality in a largely horizontal neighbourhood.

Rideau Towers. (Glenbow Archives NA–5093–447)

chapter 5

Through Subdivision Sprawl to Seamless City

Modifying the Grid: Knob Hill and Fairview

With the exception of Mount Royal and Scarboro, land subdivision during Calgary's first 60 years was based on the grid system. Far too many proposed subdivisions were registered during the frantic land boom years of 1908–12, and when the optimism evaporated, vacant tracts stretched for miles into the open countryside. Sometimes the streets were opened, utility lines and streetcar tracks laid, but mostly the face of the countryside beyond the boundaries of the pre-First World War city remained untouched. During erratic but generally slow growth through the inter-war years, these land-boom plots provided all the building sites Calgary needed.

Post-Second World War growth was initially accommodated on the previously subdivided gridiron lands. Yet this gridded pattern failed to provide enough land at central locations to accommodate schools to serve baby-boom children, while the intense demand for housing lots frequently caused shortages of parkland. The gridiron, maintain Wetherell and Kmet, was thought to have created "sterile and often unattractive" environments. It was also accused of being a "wasteful system, unable to take advantage of differing topography because of its rigid adherence to uniform lot and street widths."[1]

Pressure for new approaches to planning came from various sources. In 1945, city commissioner V.C. Newhall urged the planning commission to guarantee that future residential areas be adequately provided with schools, playgrounds and commercial sites. Two years later, the Calgary Public School Board began buying sites in advance of housing construction, ensuring that new schools were built in the most convenient locations. The provincial government's new subdivision regulations called for land dedicated to schools and parks, for maximum safety and privacy in the design of street systems and for convenient relationships among various neighbourhood elements. Nationally, the Central Mortgage and Housing Corporation became an important influence through its mandate to foster "sound community planning"; it was the first active promoter of what became known as planned unit developments.[2]

These piecemeal, largely intuitive gestures were pulled together in 1951 by A.G. Martin, the city's new planning director. Martin advocated the "neighbourhood unit" concept as the basis for spatial and functional organization of suburban development. "Such a unit would be the area reasonably served by the average elementary school," he argued. Neighbourhood spirit would be fostered through "common interest in immediate local affairs." A neighbourhood should not be "invaded by major traffic streams," and must produce a "safe and healthy living environment." Martin hoped these unit areas would have ready access to thoroughfares and transit service, and that local shopping would be readily available. Such features, he concluded, would contribute to making an area a "thoroughly desirable place to live."[3]

While some postwar subdivisions were laid out on the traditional gridiron plan, Calgary's city planners soon began advocating the Neighbourhood Unit Concept. Each neigh-

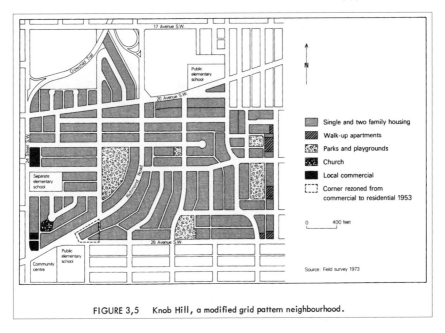

FIGURE 3,5   Knob Hill, a modified grid pattern neighbourhood.

Knob Hill. (Barr. *Calgary: Metropolitan Structure and Influence.* 1975.)

bourhood would have well-defined boundaries, residential areas
of mixed density, park space and retail shops, and a safe internal
street system with no through traffic. A centrally located school
would provide a focus for the local population. Curved streets
and irregular-shaped blocks would break the monotony of the
gridiron plan, and higher density housing, such as duplexes and
apartments, might be included in the neighbourhood.

Neighbourhood unit planning on a modified gridiron
pattern was employed initially in several areas that had long
remained undeveloped—Renfrew out of the old airport and
St. Andrews Heights on an old golf course. At the same time,
several originally gridded areas were also modified: Mountview,
Houndsfield Heights, Capitol Hill and Briar Hill. Knob Hill in

southwest Calgary was an old 1911 subdivision replotted by the city engineer's office between 1948 and 1950 on this modified gridiron pattern. Although Richmond Road split the community in half, and some right-angled corners remained, the design did include fewer through streets, several curved streets, a cul-de-sac and a crescent.

Yet disconnections are evident. No relationship was drawn between neighbourhood size and elementary school attendance areas. Neither Knob Hill (public) nor St. Charles (separate) was centrally located and their attendance areas included large sections of adjoining subdivisions. Community services included three small commercial sites—one on Richmond Road and two on 24th Street (later Crowchild Trail). These were loose clusters of individual outlets, with the expectation that convenience shoppers would walk to their nearest stores. Unfortunately, planners failed to anticipate the retailing revolution soon to burst on the city, featuring huge supermarkets and shopping centres.[5]

Fairview subdivision in southeast Calgary, designed and developed in the late 1950s, took planning principles several steps further than the Knob Hill concept. Although Fairview was one of the first privately planned neighbourhoods, its planner had previously been the city's subdivision designer and so was fully familiar with procedures and expectations of the planning board. The original Fairview shopping centre contained 12 outlets with a clear emphasis on low-order retail, personal and recreational services—a small food market, two hair stylists and a bowling alley. Soon, however, a major supermarket chose a more convenient site at Heritage and Fairmount drives, where the arterial street separating Fairview and Acadia neighbourhoods intersects with the major internal collector street. This supermarket tended to drain away ancillary services that might otherwise have located in the Fairview centre.[6]

Planning goals for providing neighbourhood stores had not

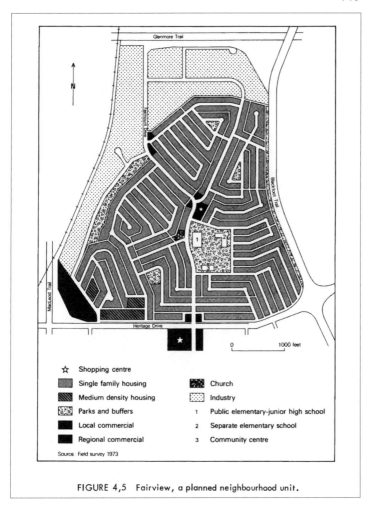

FIGURE 4,5 Fairview, a planned neighbourhood unit.

Fairview. (Barr. *Calgary: Metropolitan Structure and Influence.* 1975.)

yet been clearly thought out. In several modified gridiron areas, sites were zoned for isolated corner stores and, in some instances, shops were located on all four corners of an intersection. With this type of design, no provision was made for off-street parking

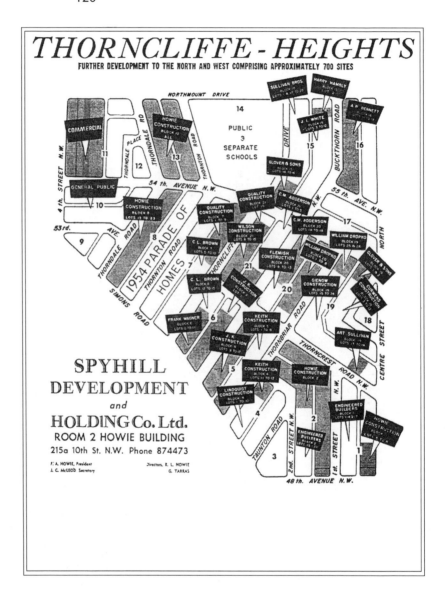

Thorncliffe Heights, 1954. *(The Calgary Herald)*

and little concern given to traffic congestion, safety or potential conflicts with adjacent housing. The policy was to zone all land having claim to commercial potential and the result was far too much commercial space. Furthermore, since all of the commercially zoned land was not developed, it either remained vacant or was absorbed by residential land uses.[7]

But there was no stopping after Knob Hill and Fairview. The city engineering department oversaw 20 major residential developments during the mid- to late-1950s, involving 856 acres (347 hectares) of land subdivided into 2,840 building sites. Britannia, Altadore, Stanley Park, Capitol Hill and Renfrew East were all launched in 1954. Lynnwood and Mountview followed

Glendale Meadows, 1958. (Glenbow Archives NA–5093–558)

Mayfair, 1958. (Glenbow Archives NA–5093–587)

the next year, Richmond Park and Cambrian Heights in 1956, and Belfast in 1958. Several major private developments were also taken over by the city during this period—Thorncliffe, Glendale, Meadowlark Park, Mountview Heights, Highwood, Highland Park and Wildwood.[8]

Belaire, planned as a high-amenity residential area in southwest Calgary, was the first to employ a laneless design. In support of this innovation, developer M.T. Ribtack argued that regular lanes are dirty and muddy, costly to maintain, and cluttered with haphazard arrays of fences, walls and poles. To ensure high quality, he was prepared to guarantee that all owners in the area would have, as part of their home, garbage disposal units, incinerators and portable carts to assist in garbage collection.[9]

Knob Hill, Fairview, Belaire: These and other postwar Calgary subdivisions were characterized by much lower densities

Eager homeowners line up to buy lots in Lynnwood subdivision, 1959.
(Glenbow Archives NA–2864–1358)

than earlier residential districts within the city. From the mid-1940s to the mid-1960s, nearly all new single-family dwellings were completely detached, surrounded on every side by their own plots. Typical lot sizes were relatively uniform, averaging between 50 by 100 and 80 by 120 feet (460 to 890 square metres). Moreover, the new subdivisions allotted a higher proportion of their land area to streets and open spaces.

Neighbourhood unit plans were "considered a sign of modernity," conclude Wetherell and Kmet. Neighbourhood planning appeared to reinforce family life by providing yards and playgrounds and safe environments for children in the new suburbs where the majority of people would soon live. This related easily to the continuing idealization of the role of the home in family life. In the heady years of postwar optimism, with an "optimism that was expressed in a yearning for stability and order and in an almost relentless acquisitiveness," desires were at least partially appeased by a house in the suburbs and by its necessary adjunct, the car.[10]

Pioneers of St. Andrews Heights

In October 1950, the *Calgary Herald* reported that construction would start early in the new year on a 1,000-unit housing development on the hill above 7th Avenue and 24th Street NW. To be developed by Campbell and Haliburton Limited, this middle- to upper-middle-class subdivision would feature single-family homes exclusively, priced from $8,000 to $12,000, all with at least three bedrooms and of varied design using various types of facing. The site would include a shopping centre and theatre, plus curved streets and dead-end avenues to protect children in a self-contained housing area.[11] Originally named Lennon Park, after former land owner George Lennon, the development remained a paper subdivision for several months, but eventually took off under the name St. Andrews Heights, honouring the site's earlier use as St. Andrews golf course.

House construction finally began in 1953, recalls Tony Usselman, a builder and long-time St. Andrews Heights resident. "The first three builders were Nu-West Homes, Quality Construction and Keith Construction. I started up Quality Construction, and had about thirty-five starts by the spring of 1954. I then incorporated my own company, Built-Rite Construction, and ended up selling shares to Alfred Hill. We worked as a good team and, by a rough guess, built almost half the houses in St. Andrews."

Construction problems faced Usselman and other builders. Access was limited to a winding gravel road, running up 33rd Street from Parkdale. "A good portion of the south and east part of the subdivision was coarse riverbed gravel in which cars and trucks would get stuck. Most of the north half of the district was a fine textured sand. When the wind blew, and blow it did, the shifting sand reminded us of travel by camel. Working conditions were rugged in the first few years since pre-servicing of lots was unheard of then. There were no sidewalks and even sewer and water lines were installed after houses reached advanced stages."[12]

Autumn 1953 saw the first families move into St. Andrews Heights, into houses scattered along 11th and 12th avenues. "Water lines were not yet connected," wrote community historian Audrey Miklos, so contractors supplied water from Parkdale. "Problems began at the end of the day, when the men finished work, because that is when the water supply also ended. The first

Looking north across Parkdale with St. Andrews Heights in right centre, 1957. Foothills Hospital is still a dream. (Glenbow Archives NA–5093–416)

Christmas saw the newly connected water line break and once again, residents of St. Andrews Heights were without water." Electricity was also an off and on affair. St. Andrews Heights was one of only two districts in Calgary with underground cable, and many problems were encountered. "Dinner was often a disaster due to power failure," Miklos remembered.[13]

Paved streets and sidewalks arrived months after families moved into their new homes. The wait for telephones was long as well, while mail was picked up at a centrally located base. For some time, the nearest bus stop was at 5th Avenue and 24th Street. "This proved quite an excursion for young mothers, especially if they had to push a stroller over the rocky path down the hill from Toronto Crescent." The area south of 14th Avenue was called the Rock Pile. Great loads of rock were removed from this area and the remainder covered with loam. Not so for the area north of 14th Avenue, referred to as the Sand Hill. "The strong winds that favour Calgary made the ever-changing sand dunes an exciting place for children to play," recalled Miklos. "The routine shakedown of sand-filled children was mothers' lot for many years."[14]

Miklos summarized St. Andrews Heights as an "island unto its own," in its early years, surrounded by open space. "To the west (Foothills Hospital site) was a large slough, which attracted small birds, partridge, ducks and deer. After freeze up, the slough became the community skating rink. Come spring, the area came alive with wild flowers. Sunsets seen from this area were breathtaking. The area north of St. Andrews Heights consisted of grazing land with a few old farmsteads."[15]

Controversy accompanied the naming of the neighbourhood's public elementary school in the mid-1950s. Provisionally called Kingston Street School, the name was altered by the Calgary Board of Education to honour Crowfoot, the illustrious Blackfoot chief. Residents, however, had not been consulted about this change and a community meeting, numbering 47 or 100, as var-

University Heights, 1962. (Glenbow Archives NA–2864–1906)

iously reported, forwarded their objections to the school board. The press had a field day with the controversy, quoting (or misquoting) various people, while charges of prejudice filled the air. In the end, the school was called Chief Crowfoot and opened with great fanfare in November 1955, with Crowfoot's grandson, Chief Joe Crowfoot, as guest of honour. The chief said he was proud to present the school with his grandfather's portrait, and hoped that "when my grandchildren are old enough they will attend Chief Crowfoot School."[16]

With the school opening and formation of a community

association, the future looked promising for St. Andrews Heights in 1955. Yet the proposed shopping centre and theatre were never built, while the Calgary Separate School Board eventually sold its site. Upscale St. Andrews Heights, like more modest Knob Hill and Fairview, was basically too small to support most public-sector services and private-sector businesses. In St. Andrews Heights, even the public school eventually closed down—long before it had any opportunity to educate Chief Joe Crowfoot's grandchildren.

Outline or Sector Planning

By the early 1960s, Calgary planners shifted their attention from neighbourhoods like St. Andrews Heights to much larger geographical units. Newer, larger outline or sector planning was intended to control expansion and facilitate "smooth development" by developing residential and service areas on an extremely vast scale. Outline or sector planning would provide a general framework into which specific development proposals could be fitted while creating a community service unit larger and more realistic than the neighbourhood. To provide identity and shape, communities would be organized around major service nodes featuring shopping centres, high schools and libraries, churches and social service clinics, fire and police stations, and entertainment facilities.[17]

The sector concept of residential planning was made explicit in Calgary's first General Plan adopted by city council in 1963. Schedules to the plan included statements of development principles for four large areas known as sectors, ranging in size from 942 to 3,185 acres (382 to 1,290 hectares), with proposed populations from 20,000 to 50,000. A sector was described as "the statement of an overall concept for the development of a geographic area of the city into an integrated community unit, which is usually bounded by such natural or man-made physical barriers as rivers, escarpments, railways or freeways."[18]

The area of southwest Calgary south of Glenmore Lake was an early example of sector planning—some 2,050 acres (830 hectares) with a projected population of between 30,000 and 48,800. The first major subdivision, Braeside, was approved in 1962. Retail services were largely concentrated at the sector centre, that is at the major intersection within the sector, while local or neighbourhood centres would be located at lesser intersections. A division of responsibility emerged, with entrepreneurs determining the number of shopping centres and city planners deciding how they would fit into residential areas they were to serve.[19]

The Glenmore Sector demonstrated several traits of classic

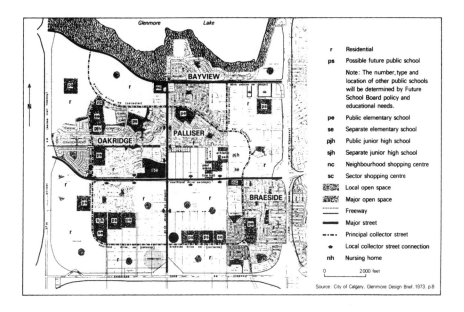

Glenmore design brief. (Barr. *Calgary: Metropolitan Structure and Influence.* 1975.)

suburban development. Large developers assembled a huge tract of land, planned the new suburb, financed the required services with their own money, then either sold lots to small house builders or (more likely) kept them and built houses themselves. Novel street layouts abandoned traditional right-angled grid systems for maze-like patterns of curving streets, discouraging through traffic and channelling it onto high-capacity arterial roads outside the development. Larger lots featured single-storey bungalows, broadside to the street and fully detached. To simplify production methods and reduce design fees, most large developers offered no more than a half-dozen basic house plans, resulting in a "monotony and repetition that was especially stark in the early years of the subdivision," before individual owners transformed their homes and yards according to personal taste. [20]

Informed by the optimism and buoyancy of the 1960s, sector planning was expected to produce rational urban development and, like neighbourhood planning before it, protect "property values through the creation of residential areas of lasting social and monetary value." Advocates believed that each community should be a microcosm of society. It was hoped that suburban residential life would be more organic, more private and yet more integrated at a local level. In physical terms, these suburbs looked different, as pedestrian walkways connected parts of the community and houses were sometimes turned around to face walkways and open spaces rather than streets. [21]

In the two decades after the Second World War, expansion occurred principally in the north and northwest, between the valleys of the Bow River and Nose Creek, and in the south along two axes, the Elbow River and Macleod Trail. Beginning in 1967, development of the Lake Bonavista neighbourhood, a high-income area in the southeast between Macleod Trail and the Bow River, marked a deviation from historical patterns. Since the site boasted no distinctive physical features, urbanist George Nader

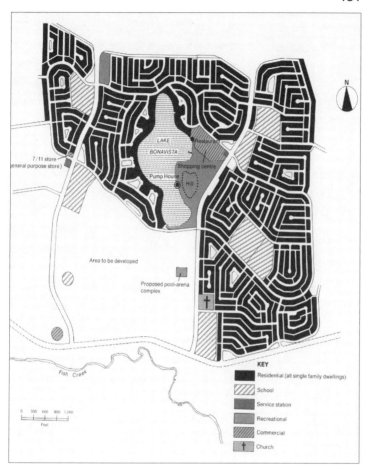

Lake Bonavista. (Baine. *Calgary: An Urban Study.* 1973.)

calls it an "excellent example of the ability of large real estate developers to alter the normal pattern of development." [22] Lake Bonavista featured a 52-acre (21-hectare) artificial lake, with the excavated earth used to build a hill that became an integral part of the community's recreational centre.

Between 1948 and 1965, over 60,000 homes were constructed, making Calgary one of the nation's leaders in single-family housing.[23] Humphrey Carver's postwar projections for suburban Canada had envisaged communities composed of three or four neighbourhoods with a total population of around 20,000. With sector planning in the area south of Glenmore Lake calling for approximately twice that population, however, Calgary moved far beyond Carver's modest figures. "Suburbia, with its earlier promises of comfort, security and a strong sense of locality," conclude Wetherell and Kmet, "had become giganticism."[24]

And giganticism encouraged consolidation in the house-construction and subdivision-development businesses in Calgary. Between 1956 and 1965, some 26,800 residential lots were developed by private developers. Kelwood Corporation developed 9,296 (34.7 percent) of those lots, followed by Carma Developers with 4,525 (16.9 percent), Spyhill Developments with 2,766 (10.3 percent), Glenmore Developments with 1,335 (5 percent), Calgary Suburban Developments with 835 (3.1 percent), with another 44 smaller operators sharing the remainder. Through the late 1950s, Kelwood was most active in Acadia, Chinook Park, Eagle Ridge, Fairview, Glendale, Haysboro, Highwood, Kingsland, Mayfair and Wildwood; Spyhill in Brentwood, Collingwood and Thorncliffe; Glenmore Developments in Lincoln Park; and Nu-West/Carma in Charleswood, Rosemont and Westgate.[25]

Carma Construction, formed as a co-operatively owned land developer in 1958 by a group of about 45 investors, focussed first on Rosemont, then Westgate. Carma became dominant in the northwest with the development of the new University of Calgary campus in the early 1960s, developing and building on more than 1,500 lots in Charleswood, Charleswood Heights, Foothills Estates, University Heights and Varsity Acres, in addition to work elsewhere in the city. By the time of its 40th anniversary in 1998, Carma had created, or helped create, some 50 Calgary communities in Alberta—from far-flung Abbeydale and Beddington to Wood-

How Streets Were Named in Postwar Calgary

Initially, no clear policy was followed in choosing names for neighbourhood streets when patterns departed from the numbered streets and avenues of the old gridiron. Knob Hill, for example, has Osborne Crescent, named after a former city mayor, and Tecumseh Road, named for nearby Tecumseh Naval Training Station. When Britannia was established in 1953, the year of Queen Elizabeth II's coronation, streets received names like Imperial Way, etc. In the Briar Hill neighbourhood, names of trees such as Juniper, Sumac and Hawthorn were chosen.

To ease the problem of determining where a street was located, particularly for police and fire-protection reasons, the Technical Planning Board ruled in 1955 that each street name in a subdivision would begin with the same letter as the subdivision name. Yet Highwood and Haysboro were in opposite ends of the city, and street names in both began with the letter "H." In 1958, the board recommended that no duplication of subdivision initials be allowed within a quadrant and that all addresses have quadrant designations. Later, all streets in a subdivision had to have their first three letters identical to that of the subdivision's name.

bine and Woodlands in the distant southwest—containing some 160,000 lots. The *Herald* estimated that "almost one in five Calgarians lives on land developed by Carma."[26]

Critics who view suburbs as an evil conspiracy between land developers and politicians, and see suburbanites as victims, perhaps fail to notice that many people who can afford to live anywhere choose to live in the suburbs. New suburbs offered families more control over where and how they lived. Young

How Subdivisions Were Named

The choice of a neighbourhood name was initially made by the Town Planning Commission and later by the developer. Yet what rhyme or reason was there? In 1951, Alderman Mary Dover objected to Briar Hill as the name for a new subdivision west of Hounsfield Heights, saying "there wasn't a briar in the area and that a good Indian name would be more suitable." But as the *Herald* pointed out in a May 3 editorial: there was no hill in Hillhurst, no park in Bonnybrook Park, no terrace in Regal Terrace and neither roses nor dales in Rosedale.

couples and mature families alike acquired freedom as house buyers, shoppers and car owners. Many acquired unprecedented amounts of privately owned space.

Housing seems to have been the main determinant. What general characteristics the suburban population possessed were related, directly or indirectly, to the fact that it "was the search for a house which determined the move to the suburbs." Many families moved from the inner city because they found residence there unpleasant, others because they could not find a downtown house they could afford. "People bought the type of house they required and could afford," concludes sociologist S.D. Clark, and it was the availability of such a house that determined *where* they bought.[27]

On the Margins of Modernism

Calgary's population tripled in the quarter-century following the Second World War, from some 100,000 in 1945 to about 400,000 in 1970. At the same time, the city's geographic area grew by the sustained and deliberate annexation of suburban lands and fringe communities. The early postwar years saw housing and small-scale developments proliferate on Calgary's margins or fringes. From 1946 to 1955, Bowness grew from 650 to 5,881 persons, Montgomery mushroomed from 60 houses in 1947 to 1,069 in 1956, while Forest Lawn's postwar population nearly doubled by 1952 and had tripled by 1954.

Construction beyond the city's geopolitical boundaries proved increasingly attractive during these years. On the fringes, as opposed to inside city limits, home owners and contractors could build on unserviced lots; housing was generally below city standards, consisting of homes without basements and lacking water and sewer connections; smaller builders could arrange low down-payments on smaller-sized houses than the National Housing Act and CMHC permitted. Lacking any effective government programs to assist low income earners to purchase city housing, those who could not or did not want to rent, maintain Wetherell and Kmet, "often took the time honoured option of the urban poor in Alberta and moved to a fringe community."[28]

Yet in most of these fringe communities, standards of public services were lower and more expensive than in the city. Tax bases were particularly narrow, with residential property poorer in quality and scarcely any revenue-generating commercial or industrial properties. Local councils often found themselves in financial difficulties and heavily dependent on provincial grants for many types of amenities. Calgary's 1955 per capita municipal expenditures were $92.91, compared with $42.72 in Forest Lawn and $27.73 in Bowness. At the same time, city planners viewed the fringes as a potential threat to orderly development, health authorities saw water and sewage problems as potentially threatening, and city accountants feared them as serious potential liabilities.[29]

Early attempts by residents of fringe communities to join

Calgary failed. Both Albert Park (1946) and Rosscarrock (1952) were well-developed residential territories, though considered "sub-standard" in terms of housing quality, service supply and financial liability. These and other petitions were strongly opposed by the City of Calgary—and subsequently turned down by the provincial annexation board—on grounds that land supply

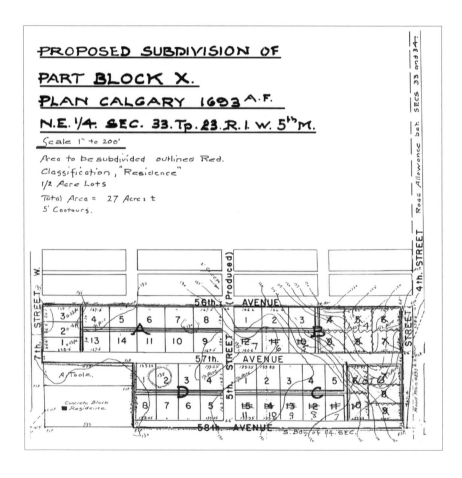

Proposed Windsor Park subdivision. (City of Calgary Archives, map 001259)

within the city was adequate for several years, that it would be too costly to extend sewer and water utilities into the new areas, plus the "impression that these suburban residents bought their homes to escape city taxes, but once the tax differential disappeared they wanted the extra services of city residents."[30] Yet annexation petitions from Windsor Park (1951), Manchester (1952) and Meadowlark Park (1955) were not opposed by the city. These neighbourhoods were judged closer to the city core and in areas experiencing growth pressures, suggesting that the city's view of logical growth areas for the immediate future would prevail over local concerns.

Meanwhile, Calgary itself became proactive, launching a successful bid in 1953 to add a large area north of the city boundaries. This application was motivated by a shortage of reasonably priced land for building contractors and developers, combined with the city's desire to simplify procedures for servicing residential areas and increase control over such development. A quarter section to the west and a full section to the north were swallowed in 1954, followed by a much larger area to the north in 1955 that allowed for expansion of the Calgary Airport. This was followed by a major annexation to the south and west in 1956, also initiated by the city's appetite for additional land and its desire to control residential, commercial and industrial development along Highway 2 south.

During the following decade, Calgary's annexations went beyond sparsely settled fringe areas to include incorporated municipalities with populations, ambiences and histories of their own. The town of Forest Lawn was gobbled up by the city in 1961 as part of a huge annexation and amalgamation of lands to the north, east and south. These particular lands, it was argued, were logical areas for urban expansion and should be developed in accordance with overall city planning. It was obvious that the city could not serve some of this vast area with sewers, roads,

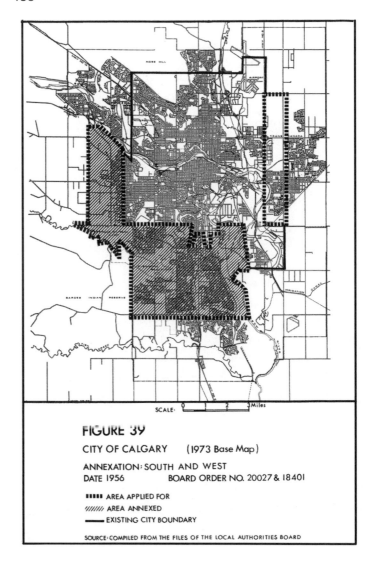

SCALE: 0   2   3 Miles

FIGURE 39

CITY OF CALGARY   (1973 Base Map)

ANNEXATION: SOUTH AND WEST
DATE 1956   BOARD ORDER NO. 20027 & 18401

▪▪▪▪▪ AREA APPLIED FOR
/////// AREA ANNEXED
▬▬▬ EXISTING CITY BOUNDARY

SOURCE: COMPILED FROM THE FILES OF THE LOCAL AUTHORITIES BOARD

Annexation, 1956. (Diemer. *Annexation and Amalgamation in the Territorial Expansion of Edmonton and Calgary.* 1974.)

lights, and fire and police protection for years to come. However, not to annex would cause greater difficulty, for small peripheral communities would grow, duplicating services and planning, and growing at cross purposes with the city. The longer this went on, the more difficult it would be to correct.

Forest Lawn, incorporated as a village in 1934 and a town in 1953, was now home to about 10,000 residents. While town council vigorously opposed joining Calgary, amalgamation was supported by residents and businesses wanting the benefits of modern services, and by developers eyeing land for middle- and low-income housing. Ultimately, the provincial annexation board ruled in favour of Calgary on December 30, 1961. All utilities would be provided at the same rates throughout the city; all debts and liabilities of the town would be assumed by the city; all public services would be raised to city standards; all Calgary bylaws would become effective in the town.[31]

Forest Lawn, 1958. (Glenbow Archives NA–5093–567)

Montgomery, 1963. (Glenbow Archives NA–2864–544)

Calgary then moved westward toward Montgomery and Bowness. Montgomery, incorporated in 1958 and with a population of about 5,000 in the early 1960s, was completely hemmed in, leaving little room to grow, while boundaries between town and city seemed totally arbitrary. In addition, it had no industry and little likelihood of attracting any, creating an imbalance between residential and commercial/industrial assessment that drove up property taxes while lowering the town's credit rating. Groups and individuals in Montgomery had long wished to amalgamate with Calgary, forwarding six petitions to the city between 1951 and 1963, the last one actually initiated by town council. With support at last from the City of Calgary, the provincial board approved amalgamation on June 14, 1963. [32]

Bowness was older than Forest Lawn and Montgomery, tracing its roots back to Bowness Park and streetcar lines in the days before the First World War, thus giving it a stronger and more-rooted identity. The community boomed in the years following the Second World War, incorporating as a village in 1948 and a town four years later, and was home to some 9,000 to 10,000 residents by the early 1960s. Bowness boasted sewer and water services, all manner of retail stores, its own shopping centre, Lions Club and newspaper, and even a hotel and two movie theatres—the Rex and the Bow. [33]

Yet like Forest Lawn and Montgomery, Bowness was burdened with an unbalanced tax base with little prospect of industrial development. Ratepayers desired Calgary police and fire protection; they expected lower transit fares and savings in utility rates and insurance premiums. They, too, wanted to be modern. A plebiscite of Bowness residents favoured amalgamation 1,003 to 197, and was supported by town council in January 1964. The Local Authorities Board approved on July 2, claiming the town was socially and economically part of Calgary. [34]

Suddenly, there were no suburbs. With the annexation of Forest Lawn, Montgomery and Bowness, Calgary became a city without suburbs—a quintessentially modern, seamless city. This allowed one municipal authority to control and streamline its approach to subdivision development. By annexation and amalgamation, Calgary gained complete control over its contiguous and metropolitan development, as well as a considerable power over land on which development would likely occur in the future. True, there remained a number of scattered housing tracts and small holdings beyond the city's corporate limits, especially to the west toward Cochrane, but except for the Spy Hill Penitentiary and Sarcee Indian Reserve, Calgary by the mid-1960s had no major peripheral developments that would hinder its future growth.

Unlike Edmonton, with its satellite communities of St. Albert and Sherwood Park, Stony Plain and Fort Saskatchewan, metropolitan Calgary had become a much more concentrated single-municipality entity. Calgary remains today one of the few large Canadian cities where the entire urbanized area comes under a single jurisdiction—the ultimate streamlined, modern metropolis.

"Don't give a dam about Bearspaw—I'm ready for a flood right now!" *(The Calgary Herald)*

chapter 6

Living the Modern Life

Shopping in the Suburbs

Shopping followed shoppers to their new homes in far-flung city neighbourhoods. "Calgary within the next ten years can expect a shift in retail buying from the downtown area to the bright new shopping districts in the suburbs," predicted Frank Cox, an American business-development consultant at a 1953 meeting of the Calgary Chamber of Commerce. New stores, reflecting latest developments in retail store design, would have "glamorous exteriors to catch the eye, superior interior lighting and store fixtures, and wide aisles to accommodate customers." Music would be heard everywhere in the stores and trained personnel would be ready to wait on shoppers. When this development occurred, it would "rip the shingles off" many businesses in the downtown area.

Shopping must cater to an automobile-oriented suburbanite. The basic cause of the trend to suburban malls, added Cox, was the "acute parking problem in downtown areas" which followed the rise in urban populations and unprecedented increases in vehicles on city streets. Shoppers found it so difficult to park their cars that they were "unwilling to drive downtown," leaving the way open for promoters to develop new shopping centres in areas where

Strip shops advertisement. *(The Calgary Herald.)*

parking problems were less acute. Cox predicted that suburban shopping centres would offer six times the parking space available in downtown Calgary.[1]

Even before the end of the 1950s, many of Calgary's most eye-catching commercial architectural developments occurred, not downtown in "high style" buildings, but at the ill-defined edge of the city—along arterial roadways, in neighbourhood shopping centres, and in huge sector and regional merchandising malls. Along Macleod Trail, for example, from 34th south to 90th Avenue, the number of businesses tripled between 1951 and 1963.

Of 120 commercial establishments by the latter date (excluding Chinook Centre), 89 of them (almost 75 percent) were highway or automotive related: gas stations, restaurants, motels, auto repair and accessory shops, and automobile, truck or trailer sales. By the 1960s, Macleod Trail had been transformed from highway-out-of-town to one of Canada's "most lively, successful and visually engaging commercial strips" dedicated to that "key component of any Calgarian's identity, the automobile."[2]

Macleod Trail took on the appearance of the generalized American strip, similar to "from Mississauga to Mississippi," argues architectural critic Trevor Boddy, boasting "some of the best, or at least some of the most extreme, Canadian examples of a new vernacular architecture," that marked this automobile culture. Boddy was particularly intrigued by the Flamingo Motel—"the thirty-foot pink flamingo and the neon-covered futuristic concrete pylon of the motel take to the stream of Macleod Trail traffic like a duck to water"—and Johnny Rocket's Car Wash—"something produced by a collaboration of Buck Rogers with Werner von Braun's V-2 team," a "grand if overly literal monument to Space Age realism." This "symbolically rich formfulness" and the "brash and fearless plundering" of architectural history along the Macleod Trail, concludes Boddy, "form a neat counterpoint to the austere developments in high architecture of the period."[3]

Yet Macleod Trail suffered disadvantages common to all North American shopping facilities strung out along arterial roadways. Customers had to hunt for parking spaces, cross a busy highway and walk in dismal surroundings for long stretches. Businesses offered poor shopping conditions and a depressing atmosphere. Such arterial strips like Macleod Trail did, however, in the words of architectural critic Victor Gruen, "succeed beautifully in the step-by-step deterioration of the surrounding residential areas by their appearance, their noise, their smells, [and] their traffic congestion."[4]

Against this backdrop of strip-development consumerism,

Haysboro Plaza, 1959. (Glenbow Archives NA–5093–780)

Calgary also welcomed planned, integrated shopping centres. Britannia, approved in 1953, was Calgary's first neighbourhood centre developed as a unit, and served as a model for Cambrian Heights, Haysboro, Mayland Heights and Stadium shopping centres. These modest *neighbourhood* shopping facilities were usually located at the junction of two major streets or collector roads. They ranged up to six acres (2.4 hectares) in size, provided up to 30,000 square feet (2,787 square metres) of leased space, were usually anchored by a supermarket and were designed to provide food and other convenience goods of daily living.

Next in size were *sector* shopping centres like Brentwood Village Mall, usually located at the junctions of major streets and expressways, and serving wider areas of the city. They occupied approximately eight acres (3.2 hectares), offered 90,000 leasable

Shoppers at Dominion Store, North Hill, 1958. (Glenbow Archives NA–2864–1854–a)

square feet (8,360 square metres) and usually boasted a junior department store as principal tenant. Largest of all were *regional* shopping centres, located at the junction of expressways and major transit corridors, sprawling over 30 or more acres (12 hectares) and boasting a minimum gross leasing space of 300,000 square feet (27,867 square metres). With one or more major department stores as principal tenants, they offered consumer goods in depth and variety, and came closest to reproducing shopping facilities once available only in downtown Calgary.

Simpsons-Sears North Hill was the city's first regional shopping centre in 1958. The site at 16th Avenue and 14th Street NW was chosen because of its location at the intersection of two major thoroughfares, and because it was central to a large and expanding residential area in the northern section of the city.

North Hill Centre, 1958. (City of Calgary Archives, photo CalA PP–00105)

North Hill Centre signalled a revolutionary approach to life and shopping by moving goods away from the downtown and out to the suburbs where people lived. It provided one-stop shopping—and a huge parking lot.[5]

But Chinook Centre soon topped everything. Located at the intersection of Glenmore and Macleod trails, on land formerly occupied by the Chinook Drive-In Theatre (itself a modernist icon), Western Canada's largest shopping mall opened in August 1960 with a Woodward's department store and 44 other retailers. "Springtime Prevails Permanently; Even Temperatures, No Dust or Draft" promised a newspaper advertisement heralding the arrival of the enclosed, climate-controlled mall. Three years later, Southridge Shopping Centre opened just north of Chinook with Sears, Loblaws and 33 other tenants. The two centres came under joint ownership in the 1970s, and were linked by a 42-store bridge spanning 60th Avenue. Through several later expansions, Chinook Centre remained Calgary's largest and most popular mall.[6]

North Hill and Chinook centres differed markedly from downtown retailing and became temples of consumerism in the modernist era. People travelled to them, not on foot or by public transit, but by private automobile. Stores were moved off the street so that, instead of having frontage on a public sidewalk and roadway, they opened onto a privately owned mall. Retail businesses were no longer property owners, owning the store they occupied, or tenants paying a fixed monthly rental, but concessionaires who shared profits with landlords. Shopping centres depended not on local merchants but on large retail chains, particularly supermarkets and department stores, to attract consumers. They did much more than provide the kind of local shopping facilities traditional for neighbourhood shopping districts.

North Hill and Chinook attracted the kind of retail

Retail Sales at Calgary Shopping Centres in 1966			
Type of Store	Neighbourhood Centre e.g. Britannia	Sector Centre e.g. Brentwood	Regional Centre e.g. Chinook
Food	67.5%	20.0%	12.2%
Drug	7.0	1.3	.07
Clothing	2.9	6.0	6.9
Other	22.6	72.7	80.2
Ownership			
Independent	37.4	15.9	9.4
Chain	62.6	84.1	90.6
G. A. Nader, Cities of Canada. 1975.			

businesses that had previously gone downtown, and substantially weakened the dominance of central-core business over local markets. By 1966, downtown Calgary accounted for only 25 percent of the city's retail sales, a proportion much lower than its sister prairie cities of Edmonton and Winnipeg. In his study of major Canadian cities, George Nader concluded that, by 1969, Calgary had the highest ratio of planned shopping centres to metropolitan population: 9.0 square feet per person compared to 6.2 for Toronto.[7]

A Schooling in Modernism

Calgary Herald reporter Jocelyn Sara could hardly contain her excitement as she prepared a feature story on the 1947 opening of a 12-room addition to Glengarry Elementary School at 19th Avenue and 29th Street SW. Sara was particularly impressed with the school's "streamlined design, its brightness through special window arrangements and sky-lights, and the delicate and varied colour schemes in each classroom," summing the building up as an "interior decorator's dream and an architect's prize piece." When completed, the school would be the first in the Calgary Board's large postwar building program, as well as the "most modern in Western Canada."[8]

So the great postwar school-building boom began. "We were so busy providing accommodation, we had to run fast just to stand still," recalled school superintendent Robert Warren. "Most of our energies were spent just keeping up with the population. We were opening new classrooms at the rate of about three a week. We had to equip the room, we had to get a teacher for the room, we had to reorganize schools and all that type of thing." Added school trustee P.P.C. Haigh: "Sometimes the difficulty was that you'd build a nine-room school and before the school was finished you'd have to make it sixteen rooms. This happened in many places.

Classroom interior, Henry Wise Wood High School. (Glenbow Archives NA–5093–1012)

When we built Richmond, a very fine survey was made in June as to the enrollment the following September. It was way short. That was the story of those years."[9]

The story was driven by young married couples and their children. Like suburbs across North America, new housing developments in Calgary were composed largely of adults of child-bearing age and their children, initially quite young. In southwest Calgary in 1961, 39 percent of the population were between 25 and 44, while just three percent were over 55. There were only two age groups, argues historian Douglas Owram, and they were sharply defined: parents of child-bearing age, and "overwhelming even the numbers of home-owners," the children themselves. More than one-third, and sometimes nearly half, of Canada's suburban population was made up of children 14 or under in 1961.[10]

New schools had to be built. As veterans and newly married couples moved into their postwar dream homes in the subdivisions,

Kensington Road School. (Glenbow Archives NA–2864–1588)

schools were not far behind. After Glengarry received its addition in 1947, three brand-new schools opened the following year— Manchester, Bow View (later Kensington Road) and Mount View. Queen's Park followed the next year, then Richmond in 1950. But this was just the beginning. The late 1950s welcomed eight new schools annually; by 1960, the Calgary public board had opened 58 new schools since the end of the Second World War.

These postwar schools looked decidedly different than the "high-noon Gothic" of Calgary's old sandstone schools. "There was a different kind of building for homes," recalled trustee Haigh, and "since schools generally reflect the homes, we changed to the horizontal sprawling design." Consisting of one storey and built of brick and stucco with a multitude of windows, these new structures were of advanced steamlined modern design. Teacher Phyllis Weston loved the "newest type of lighting, pastel-coloured walls, floors covered with heavy linoleum," plus built-in cupboards and bookcases that removed these structures from the "traditional schoolhouse of the earlier period."[11]

By the mid-1960s, a few Calgary school building projects transcended the streamlined moderne of horizontal sprawl to approach High Modernist design. Mayland Heights Elementary School of 1967 (Gordon Atkins Architects) takes modern architecture to an extreme. Critic Douglas Gillmor praises its "freely disposed building elements"—classrooms, library and gymnasium, both in plan and in third dimension—as contrasting more conventional grid plans and contributing to its overall organic form. Gently sloping berms around the exterior walls "give the sense of the building literally growing out of its site." Carol Moore Ede, reviewing the building in 1971, wrote: "The school is built with all of the ingenuity of one who understands the child's world."[12]

Certainly, changing approaches to children and changed programming accompanied changes in school architecture. The

Earl Grey School, showing new structure before original building was demolished.
(Glenbow Archives NA-2864-1578-10a)

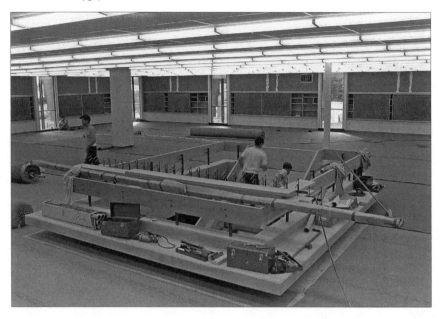

Earl Grey interior. (Glenbow Archives NA–2864–1578–9a)

Second World War focussed great faith in young people as the hope for a better world, and in the school—the one agency that reached all the children of all the people—as the institution that could guide Canadian youth through the postwar world. But how could a large school system best help individual youngsters cope with the problems of the contemporary world? How could it help students realize their full potential while still in school, to give a positive foundation for adulthood? Increasingly in the late 1940s, the Calgary Public School Board placed its faith in guidance or student counselling.

Guidance supervisor Harold Panabaker's 1946 report provided a blueprint for postwar developments in counselling. For elementary schools he advocated the "study of individual

Students Find Everything Fitted
for Individual Sizes at Schools

Going to school these days is getting to be just like entering the world of Goldilocks, for just like the three bears, the students have everything fitted to their size.

They have big desks, middle-sized desks and baby desks, and believe it or not in the new schools, it goes even further than that. At Parkdale, a 15-room elementary school which opened this fall on the Western outskirts of the city, the washrooms feature big sinks, middle-sized sinks and baby sinks—just to make keeping clean easy for everyone.

Parkdale is the largest of four schools opened by the Calgary public school board this fall. Situated at 32nd Street and 5th Avenue NW in one of the new and rapidly populating districts of Calgary.[sic]

For Parkdale students, going to school is a treat few of their parents experienced. Their classes are conducted in roomy, bright classrooms full of modern conveniences, and their teachers are young but experienced.

Parkdale is a one-storey school with space for a large playground. It's a U-shaped building finished in white stucco, and in the centre of the U is a stone court yard which is used as a play space.

Double green doors open from the court yard into two large playrooms which may be used when weather is unpleasant. Running through the centre of the building is a spacious hall with a dull red floor specially constructed to deaden noise, and walls are finished in pale green. The ceilings are acoustic tile.

Along each of the two arms of the building are the classrooms, each one finished in a different pastel colour. All have lots of cupboard space, a project table, a sink for the students and a private cloakroom. In the Grade 1 room, there is even an electric fireplace for use in winter.

For the most part, students work in diffused natural light, which is deflected from the venetian blinds on to the sloping ceiling. So no one, teacher or students, has to face a blinding glare when the sun is high.

The air in each room comes directly from the outside, circulated through the room and passed outside again through a special unit. Its temperature is controlled through a thermostat, and it is always fresh.

The back of the building is centred by a gymnasium with a large stage and a kitchen for use at school teas and parties. The music room is also the school library.

The kindergarten room is spacious and cheery with an electric fireplace and large cloakroom facilities. It is the only room in the school with private washrooms for both boys and girls.

The building cost $307,090, and principal R.B. Walls wants to "get our money's worth of good out of the school."

—*Calgary Herald*, October 6, 1952

differences and the modification of curriculum, instruction, and treatment" to meet individual needs; continuous effort to discover "special difficulties and weaknesses" of individual pupils and then provide instruction necessary to "remove the difficulties" or the treatment necessary to overcome the weaknesses; early discovery of children who, "because of physical defects, home conditions, or poor environment," show symptoms of emotional disturbances; continued and increasing emphasis upon the creation and maintenance of a "wholesome emotional atmosphere" in all classrooms. Such strategies should continue in junior and senior high schools, recommended Panabaker, plus standardized tests of intelligence, aptitudes, interests and emotional adjustment; individual counselling for all students who wished; detailed and accurate information on the world of work; and job-placement and follow-up assistance for students leaving school.[13]

For many critics, out of step with modernist educational thinking, guidance was just another example of a softening-up or watering-down of the hard realities of life. Like schools across the country, Calgary classrooms during these postwar years replaced kings-of-England history and place-name geography with the supposedly more relevant subject called "social studies." Project-oriented, child-centred learning elbowed aside drill and rote

Gridded University of Calgary campus, 1964. (University of Calgary Archives)

memorization. Junior high schools eased the transition from elementary to high school. By the 1960s, vocational programs in senior highs competed strongly for students and money with traditional academic programs. Such streamlining of the educational process, easing transitions from level to level, was central to the modernist educational ethos.

Thousands of teachers for these new schools, and for the new modernist approaches, were trained at the city's infant university. The University of Calgary traces its roots back to the old Calgary Normal School, founded in the early years of the 20th century, and transformed in 1945 into the Calgary Branch of the University of Alberta. This move from normal school to provincial university was hailed as a "modern programme for the preparation of teachers,"[14] and fundamentally changed the institution then sharing quarters with the Provincial Institute of Technology. The Calgary Branch added to its education base with programs in arts and science, commerce and engineering; renamed itself the University of Alberta at Calgary; moved to its present campus in 1960; and gained full autonomy as the University of Calgary in 1966.

Temples of Modernism

With shopping chores completed and younger children under the care of trusted baby sitters, Calgarians during the last week of April 1957 donned their best duds for an evening—or several evenings—at their new modernist entertainment shrine.

From suburban tract houses and inner-city walk-ups, they flocked to performances of symphony and musical comedy, ballet and opera, drama and pageant, at the magnificent new Southern Alberta Jubilee Auditorium. Three years earlier, Alberta Premier Ernest Manning proposed two large auditoriums, one in Edmonton and one in Calgary, to commemorate the province's

Southern Alberta Jubilee Auditorium, 1957. (Glenbow Archives NA–5093–625)

50th anniversary. Designed by the provincial Department of Public Works, construction of the $4.5 million edifice began in summer 1955 on Calgary's North Hill, west of the building housing the Provincial School of Technology and Art and the fledgling Calgary Branch of the University of Alberta.

The Jubilee housed a 2,700-seat auditorium, large stage and essential backstage rooms, with reception lobbies, exhibition areas and social rooms at different levels. "Entirely free of any form of architectural pretension," boasted the provincial government, the building "makes an honest and forthright statement of its purpose, and clearly visible in the modernity and economy of its uncluttered exterior one may see the essential shape of the great fan-shaped auditorium and its high stage tower."[15]

Calgarians entered this temple of modernism through a double row of 17 glass doors opening into a foyer, where "gleaming

Jubilee Auditorium lobby. (Glenbow Archives NA–5093–350)

surfaces of Venetian terrazzo floors, marble columns, mirror-walls and wood panelling make an immediate impression of shining newness and cleanliness," with box office, checkroom, telephones and rest rooms immediately visible. Separating the foyer from the lobby was a row of beautifully matched columns of polished red marble from Italy. Mounting three shallow steps, "brightly lit and provided with a non-slip treatment for safety," patrons entered the spacious and luxurious lobby with its open promenade and furnished lounge area.[16]

Entering the main lobby, eager Calgarians were "immediately transported from the work-a-day world into an atmosphere of luxury and graceful elegance." They moved quietly, "almost floating," over rich custom-made carpeting which absorbed and checked noise. Seven brass chandeliers "shed great brilliant circles of light along the entire length of the lobby, while random-spaced lights twinkle like stars in the high ceiling." Round, fluted columns featured walnut strips over a white glossy base. Heavy gold drapes, low, flower-filled planters, the muted pastels and deep colours of

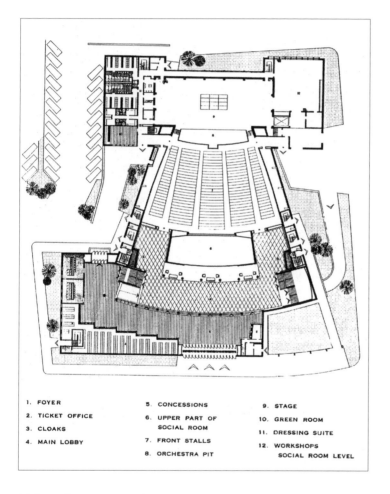

1. FOYER
2. TICKET OFFICE
3. CLOAKS
4. MAIN LOBBY

5. CONCESSIONS
6. UPPER PART OF SOCIAL ROOM
7. FRONT STALLS
8. ORCHESTRA PIT

9. STAGE
10. GREEN ROOM
11. DRESSING SUITE
12. WORKSHOPS SOCIAL ROOM LEVEL

Jubilee Auditorium seating plan. (Alberta Department of Public Works. *Jubilee Auditoriums, Edmonton and Calgary*. 1957.)

the upholstered furnishings "impart warmth, while reflections in the gleaming mirror-panelled walls at either end of the lobby bring added depth and colour to the whole scene." Yet in keeping with modernist principles, public works insisted that "nowhere is there the slightest suggestion of the ornate, the forced or pretentious design so often associated in the public mind with so impressive an interior." At the Jubilee, it was the "dignity achieved by simplicity of form, design and ornamentation."[17]

Theatre and concert goers moved effortlessly from the lobby through wide doors into the fan-shaped auditorium with its walls of polished French walnut and up broad stairways at either end to upper balcony levels. "Devoid of meaningless embellishment," the auditorium achieved much of its decorative effect through the "intrinsic beauty of its acoustical design." The sectional ceiling of large moulded plastic panels, the inward tilt of the side walls, the forceful sweep of the balcony, the random pattern of acoustic tone cabinets and perforated tiles over the carpeted and insulated rear walls, the carpeted aisles, the padded doors, the very seats, all served as "aids to acoustic perfection."[18]

What did it matter that the opening-night audience for Shakespeare's As You Like It only heard the actors if they moved near microphones concealed in stage shrubbery, or that patrons 40 years later complained of poor sight lines.[19] What counted in 1957 was that the city now boasted sumptuous accommodation for stage and musical entertainment, a new home for the recently formed Calgary Film Society and Calgary Philharmonic Orchestra. The opening of the Jubilee Auditorium, according to program notes for Bizet's Carmen, presented by the Calgary Opera Association, "marks the transformation from small town into modern city."[20]

The Jubilee did not stand alone, however, for Calgarians welcomed two other modernist leisure palaces during these postwar years—the Stampede Corral and McMahon Stadium. As profits swelled in the late 1940s, Calgary Exhibition and Stampede

Stampede Corral, 1950. (Glenbow Archives NA–5093–215)

directors committed themselves to a new hockey and general purpose arena. Construction of the $1,125,000 Corral began in May 1949, with the official opening on December 26, 1950, when 8,729 fans, the largest audience ever to see a hockey game in Western Canada, watched the Calgary Stampeders blank the Edmonton Flyers 5-0 in a Western Canada Hockey League contest.

Designed by Stevenson, Cawston & Stevenson and built by Bird Construction, the steel and concrete building featured no interior supporting pillars, thus giving each spectator an uninterrupted view of the action. A 24-foot concourse circled the building, housing concessions, offices, dressing rooms and other such features. A "completely modern" freezing plant enabled an ice sheet to be formed in 24 hours, allowing a horse show one night,

McMahon Stadium, 1960. (Glenbow Archives NA–2864–1869)

a hockey game the next. This put the Corral on a par with Maple Leaf Gardens in Toronto, and gave Calgary a building "not only modern, but as far ahead of other arenas as possible."[21]

The football Stampeders had long played their home games at Mewata Stadium in the downtown's west end. Built in 1929, Mewata no longer sufficed for the football team that won the Grey Cup in 1948 and continued to draw capacity crowds in subsequent years. Voters in May 1949 rejected a bylaw to pump $75,000 of public money into expanding the old stadium. A decade later, private money from the McMahon brothers came to the rescue. On the North Hill, just south of the new university campus, McMahon Stadium was speedily built in just 101 days during the spring and summer of 1960. The stadium officially opened on August 15, 1960, as the Stampeders hosted the Winnipeg Blue Bombers.

Meanwhile, east of the new Jubilee Auditorium, the art department of the Provincial School of Technology introduced impressionable students and often-sceptical patrons into the modern era of the visual arts. When Illingworth Kerr took over as department head in 1947, he was finally able to build up a full-time staff—Stan Perrott, Marion Nicoll, Luke Lindoe, Stan Blodgett— all advocates, in varying degrees, of modernism. Instructors did not want students "ill-prepared to face a modernized world," Kerr recalled. "We rubbed their noses in Cezanne reproductions, pointing to the infinitely complex structures that led Picasso and Bracque to invent cubism."[22]

Marion Nicoll earned a reputation as Alberta's first committed abstract artist, a teacher who believed art's main object was to widen vision. "I believe in the mission of experimental art," she boldly stated in 1953. "The painting of pictures for decoration of the walls is finished."[23] She was one of the first painters in Alberta to take up the modernist cause, argues her biographer, Christopher Jackson, and "move away from art as a re-creation of the physical world." Nicoll's work "demonstrates very clearly the modernist notion of a painting as a distinct object which exists in its own right and conforms to the necessities of painting rather than the strictures of perceptual reality."[24] By the end of 1960s, many of her students began making their own marks on the art scene, and abstraction was the norm among painters and sculptors in Calgary.

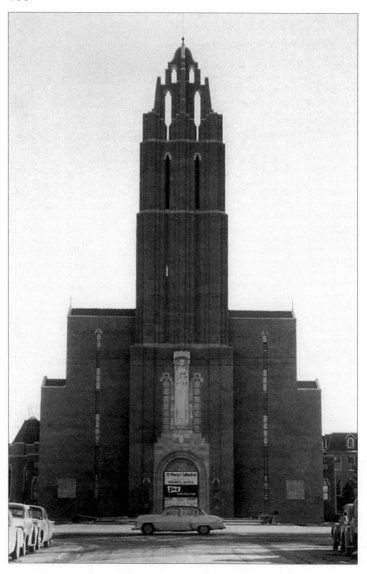

St. Mary's Cathedral, 1957. (Glenbow Archives NA–5093–305)

Sharing the spotlight with Marion Nicoll, in some respects her predecessor in shaking up the city's visual arts community, was Maxwell Bates. While his return to Calgary in January 1946 heralded modernism's arrival in the city, Bates found the local environment not all that receptive to his paintings, and he found solace in his second area of expertise—architecture. His most dramatic building was the new St. Mary's Cathedral for the Roman Catholic Diocese of Calgary, consecrated on December 11, 1957. Writing some years later, *Herald* architecture critic Stephanie White found the interior of St. Mary's "cool, quiet and very meditative." White adored the "beautifully proportioned" exterior with additions on the sides "creating a complex base to

St. Gabriel's Anglican Church. (Glenbow Archives NA–761–12a)

St. Luke's Roman Catholic Church. (Clyde McConnell)

a solid and straightforward building." She praised the "immense refinement" of the cathedral, contrasting its "classic religious hopefulness" with what she considered the "disillusioned, cynical romanticism" of Bates's paintings.[25]

New churches proliferated through the 1950s and 1960s to accommodate growing congregations in burgeoning suburban areas. St. Gabriel's Anglican Church on 30th Avenue NW (Blais & Shedden Architects) represents, according to Douglas Gillmor, the more modest end of the modern design spectrum, with three other ecclesiastical structures representing more unique expressions of modernist architecture: St. Luke's Roman Catholic Church on Northmount Drive NW (Cohos, Delesalle & Evamy); St. Andrew's United Church on Heritage Drive SW (Bill Boucock Associates); and Shaarey Tzedec Synagogue (Abugov and Sunderland) at 17th Avenue and Centre Street South.

Whether modest or unique, these and other modernist churches represented, in Gillmor's words, "a stylistic move away from the more typical, symbolic arched form toward sculptural shape and a more transcendental inner space, largely achieved through the creative manipulation of natural light."[26]

St. Luke's interior. (Clyde McConnell)

When the postwar age first dawned, back in the mushroom-gold summer of 1945, Calgarians thought themselves thoroughly modern, with their Modern Barber Shop, Modern Beauty Shoppe, Modern Café, Modern Cleaners, Modern Motors, Modern Real Estate, Modern Radio and Television Service, and so on through the telephone directory. Modern, in the sense of being up-to-date, those early postwar Calgarians certainly were. Twenty years later, however, city residents were full participants of modernism, living the modernist life in their suburban bungalows and ranch-styles, shopping at North Hill and Chinook centres, taking in games at the Stampede Corral and McMahon Stadium, studying at the new University of Calgary, worshipping at St. Mary's Cathedral, enjoying themselves at the Jubilee Auditorium. How much better could life get?

Shaarey Tzedec interior. (Glenbow Archives NA–5093–904)

chapter 7

The Limits of Modernism

A Woman's Place

"Calgary is probably as cosmopolitan as Marseilles or New York," claimed city personnel director D.R. Rees in August 1953, with the varied work force at city hall resembling "the United Nations secretariat." Rees pointed to the planning department's drafting room, which included Scandinavian, German, Hungarian and Polish-born employees, along with just two Canadian-born. Or the water department, with 145 "New Canadians" among its 345 employees: 73 Italians, 16 Hungarians, 13 Germans, 11 Ukrainians, 7 Russians, 5 Czechoslovaks, 3 Romanians, 2 Frenchmen, 2 Bulgarians, 2 Dutchmen, 1 Yugoslav, 1 Swede, 1 Austrian and 1 Latvian. However, Rees found just five New Canadians among the 50 employees of the more prestigious engineering department, and none in the police or fire departments.[1]

Blacks, Jews and women would have been even more difficult to find. Discrimination against blacks—in employment, accommodation and entertainment—was rampant in immediate postwar Calgary, leading to the formation of the Alberta Association for the Advancement of Coloured People and a 20-year struggle for equality.[2] In 1946, the Calgary Board of Education hired its first black teacher and placed her in a primary-grade classroom. City teachers, claimed Herbert Dickson, principal of Bridgeland Elementary School, were "proud of the board" for this step. Dickson naively hoped this breakthrough would improve conditions for other minorities. Why, he asked an embarrassed Junior Chamber of Commerce meeting at the Palliser Hotel in March 1947, "aren't Jews accepted at the Glencoe or the country clubs, or similar clubs?"[3]

Chinese woman and child in postwar Calgary.
(Glenbow Archives NA–4893–13)

Yet the Calgary story of minorities and modernism may best be illustrated by examining the role and influence (or lack thereof) of the city's women in the quarter century after the end of the Second World War. Once hostilities ceased, women were expected to leave the armed forces and wartime industries and return to their socially determined sphere of activity—the home. A 1944 Gallup poll indicated that 75 percent of Canadian men, as well as 68 percent of Canadian women, believed men should be given preference in postwar employment. Calgary's Local Council of Women supported this return to the home.

In addition to the Council, Calgary women were active in church groups, parent-teacher associations, the YWCA and the Alberta Council on Child and Family Welfare. Symbolic and actual gains were slow in coming. Between 1945 and 1968,

Children with Stoney Elders, 1952 Stampede. (Glenbow Archives NA–5093–20)

for example, Calgarians elected 65 aldermen to city council, only four of whom were women: Rose Wilkinson, Mary Dover, Isabella Stevens and Marion Law. And despite the multicultural boasting of personnel director D.R. Rees, city hall had a policy of not hiring married women in the postwar years. The first woman to join the Calgary Fire Department was Marlene Kroll in 1961, described in a news story as a "17-year-old brunette receptionist."[4]

Canadian media portrayals of women in the postwar years stressed "an all-pervasive stereotype of women as happy homemakers, winsome wives, and magnanimous mothers." The media did not question whether or not the normal and desired fate of most women was marriage and motherhood, argues historian Alison Prentice. Advertisements aimed at the single woman counselled her on "how to catch a man," and glamour was decreed "her most highly prized attribute." Once she had used her beauty to achieve marital status, it was a "woman's duty to continue to be sexually attractive to her husband." Yet only with her transformation into mother, however, was a woman able to "reach her full potential."[5]

Residential suburbs provided "symbolic female counterparts, bedrooms as it were, to the male-dominated, market-oriented world of modern cities," argues Veronica Strong-Boag. Tracts of new housing in Calgary and elsewhere across the country "embodied a separation of the sexes that held women particularly responsible for home and family and men for economic support and community leadership." New housing that enshrined a gendered division of labour also responded to a generation's anxiety about dangers in the world about them. The threat of the Cold War encouraged citizens to prize the private consumption and accumulation of products in the nuclear family household as proof of capitalism's success. "Suburban housewives at home in ever larger houses epitomized the promise that prosperity would guarantee both individual happiness and the final triumph over communism."[6]

Popular and academic opinion supported the belief that collective happiness and well-being were most likely when women concentrated their energies on the home front. Typical advertisements credited the housewife with upholding family and communal virtues. Magazines, radio, films and television entered households with a distinct message about the meaning of the good life, making it quite clear that "good wives and mothers stayed properly at home far from the temptation of employment."[7]

Female residents were expected and urged to bring uniqueness to suburban uniformity "through a careful attention to decoration and design." Their choice of furniture, appliances, art and even clothes was to "transform the identical into the distinguishable, in the process confirming housewives' skill and status." Practically every issue of popular Canadian women's magazines like the *Bride's Book, Canadian Home Journal, Canadian Homes and Gardens* and *Chatelaine*, not to mention their American counterparts, offered readers ways, thrifty and otherwise, to personalize suburbia.[8]

The Calgary Stampede best captured this idealized role of modern womanhood in the postwar city. Cowgirls were an integral part of the rodeo action at early Stampedes—competing in saddle-bronc, steer-roping, trick-riding and other competitions. By the postwar years, however, they had disappeared from the arena, replaced by the annual Stampede Queen as the idealized example of modern virginal womanhood. Patsy Rodgers was crowned the first Queen of the Calgary Exhibition and Stampede in 1946, and was immediately thrust into a limelight of parades and personal appearances she had never dreamed of. Fifty years later, Patsy Rodgers Henderson rode in the 1996 Stampede parade as honorary parade marshal, leading a colour party of former queens and princesses.

Responding to feminist criticism, the Stampede in 1964 established a volunteer committee to select judges and consider contest rules. The committee emphasized that choosing the annual queen was "definitely not a cheesecake competition." The girl must have an appeal—"a fresh young face to set the tone for the year." Girls would also be judged on public speaking and equestrian skills, and their ability to work with people on a one-to-one basis and with a large crowd.[9] Years later, Stampede officials continued to stress "beauty is just one small segment" of the competition. Horsemanship remained a top priority in determining winners. "You have to be able to cowboy up or else you'll be laying in the dirt."[10]

Yet *Herald* columnist Catherine Ford continued to wonder why so "much breath is expended" explaining that competitions, particularly in the case of the Stampede Queen, are "definitely

Patsy Rodgers, 1946 Stampede Queen. (Glenbow Archives NA–3127–1)

not, repeat not, beauty contests." No indeed, they are competitions for poise, grace, to be the embodiment of western spirit for a year. Why, then, asked Ford, "are the qualifications narrowed to young women from 18 to 25, who are not married and do not have children? If these young women are simply ambassadors for the Stampede and the city, why not choose a 35-year-old with four kids or a young man. Why not a Stampede King? Because the truth, despite all the explanations and good intentions, is that these women are decorations," concluded Ford. "They are on parade."[11]

Despite the glamour surrounding the Stampede Queen, increasing numbers of Calgary—and Canadian—women did not conform to the stereotype. For example, the proportion of married women among paid female workers continued to rise, until by 1961 nearly half of all female workers were married. The proportion of wives who were in the paid labour force rose from four percent in 1941 to 20 percent in 1961 to 28 percent in 1967. From the mid-1950s on, for the first time in Canadian history, the number of women entering the workforce was greater than the number of men. A dramatically falling birth-rate due to improved (and more easily accessible) contraceptives—from 28.2 births per thousand women in 1957 to 18.2 per thousand 10 years later— liberated women from the tyranny of unwanted pregnancies and eased women's move into the work force.[12]

Women's experiences were neither homogeneous nor uncomplicated, concludes Strong-Boag. They were much more than merely the female counterparts of "organization men." Women were "both victims and beneficiaries of a nation's experiment with residential enclaves that celebrated the gendered division of labour." Suburban dreams captured the hopes of a generation shaken by war and Depression, but a domestic landscape that presumed that lives could be reduced to a single ideal inevitably failed to meet the needs of all Canadians. In the

1960s the daughters of the suburbs, examining their parents' lives, "would begin to ask for more."[13]

Revenge of the Women

Through the 1950s, Calgary's Local Council of Women (LCW) focussed its attention on such worthy causes as the treatment of prisoners, conditions and rights of Indians, financial plight of widows, immigration, equal pay for equal work, child abuse and marital property laws. But the Council attracted far more media attention in the 1960s when it spearheaded opposition to the Canadian Pacific Railway's proposal to build a new set of railway tracks along the south bank of the Bow River as part of the City-CPR Downtown Redevelopment Plan. This opposition from Calgary women attacked several of modernism's central beliefs— bigger is better, the expert knows best—and helped bring down the curtain on the city's modern era.

The Council of Women's chief protagonist was undoubtedly Ruth Gorman, a city lawyer angered over the City's seeming abandonment of a commitment to an LCW proposal for a park extending along the river between the Louise and Langevin bridges. Opposing Gorman and the LCW were most of Calgary's male-dominated business community and city council, led initially by Mayor Harry Hays, elected in October 1959 with the backing of the pro-business Civic Government Association (CGA) voters' group.

On April 5, 1963, the City and the CPR unveiled a $35 million track relocation project. Calgarians learned that the existing railway right-of-way between 9th and 10th avenues would be removed, freeing 102 acres (41.3 hectares) of prime downtown land for commercial development, thus yielding an estimated $90 million in property taxes over the next two decades. Rail lines would be relocated to the south bank of the Bow, with Canadian

Pacific and Canadian National sharing a new union station near the site of old Fort Calgary. An eight-lane parkway would parallel CP's east-west tracks along the river.

The project was generally welcomed, as it offered prospects of millions of dollars of development money being spent in Calgary. It promised employment opportunities, provincial grants and the removal of downtown trackage that was always a source of tax and traffic complaints. The press and prominent businessmen sensed that Calgary was headed for a boom, with developers "waiting in the wings."[14] When asked if the proposal to run a parkway (or, more appropriately, an arterial highway) along the riverbank would be opposed, Mayor Hays replied that the "benefits so outnumber the liabilities that any thinking Calgarian will go along with it."[15]

Interestingly, the project was unveiled not at City Hall, but at "a very fine party" hosted by the CPR at the Palliser Hotel to which prominent businessmen (but no LCW reps) were invited. And it was apparent that CPR officials had greater knowledge of the project's history than did city employees. Although Mayor Hays (by this time the new federal minister of agriculture) and certain city commissioners had been involved in the year-long CPR negotiations, most aldermen and some commissioners were not privy to the same level of information. More significantly, Calgary's chief solicitor was removed from the project when his support turned lukewarm. "Truth to tell," laments LCW historian Marjorie Norris, "the agreement had been finely crafted by the CPR's legal department."[16]

From a planning point of view, however, much had changed. The glittering City-CPR plan had pre-empted the more mundane but prerequisite downtown master plan. Two weeks after the unveiling, at the April 21st council meeting, Alderman Jack Leslie successfully initiated a request for a separate economic impact study by outside consultants. With reference to LCW's concerns,

Leslie noted previous plans had called for river beautification, not railway track relocation. To him the two terms "were not synonymous." At the same time, the Council of Women reaffirmed its earlier support for a green strip, and formed a watchdog or special study committee, chaired by Ruth Gorman, charged with studying the agreement and attending City Council meetings.[17]

The City-CPR project was approved in principle at the May 23 council meeting. Council instructed commissioners to investigate economic and environmental aspects of the project, and commissioners sι bsequently hired a Montreal firm to prepare a report. As anticipated, the consultants' report endorsed the City-CPR plan. Meanwhile, council appointed a three-man committee to promote the plan to citizens. That October, Hays' candidate of choice, Grant MacEwan, won the mayorality election with CGA support. Though the new mayor also endorsed the project, he was not so privy as Hays to the contract details. Meanwhile, squabbles appeared to develop between the City and the CPR over cost-sharing.[18]

In anticipation of a spring 1964 plebiscite, several lobby groups formed. Championing the proposal were Calgarians for Progress (CFP), co-chaired by prominent oilman Carl Nickle, and the Calgary Development Committee (also headed by Nickle), representing real estate and downtown business interests. Lining up against were the Citizens for Community Development, the South Bow Bank River Property Owners' Association and the Local Council of Women.

The LCW arranged a public debate for March 9, 1964, inviting three participants from the pro side: Mayor MacEwan, CPR project manager Rod Sykes and a Calgarians for Progress representative; and three antis: a lawyer, an urban geographer and Ruth Gorman. Sykes and the CFP both declined to attend, so MacEwan came and filled the debate vacancies with two aldermen—Ted Duncan and Ernie Starr. It seemed that the City was left to defend the agreement alone, "abandoned by its partner, the CPR, and by the project's strongest advocate, the CFP."[19]

Five hundred Calgarians attended the debate, most preferring "to bury the CPR rather than praise it." In what the press described as a "searing" attack, Gorman opened the debate, urging citizens to discover document loopholes themselves. Quite unexpectedly, Mayor MacEwan discovered he did not have Alderman Ernie Starr in his firmament. "The trouble we are in today," admitted Starr, "is due to a pressure group brought in by the CPR—I'm talking about Calgarians for Progress; they've been sending out literature Council has never seen."[20] The next day the *Herald* headlined its story, "Mayor, Aldermen Booed, Hissed at Noisy City-CP Project Forum."

A May 21 front-page story galvanized the Local Council of Women. That morning, based on a telephone tip, *The Albertan* broke the news that Alderman (and architect) Dave Russell's employer had "transferred" him out of Calgary to open a Kelowna branch of Rule, Wynne & Rule Associates.[21] The firm's senior partner admitted to pressure from clients who favoured the CPR plan, and balked at Russell's opposition. Russell refused the move, and was dismissed. "When this information leaked into the newspapers, citizens, especially the women in our organization, were shocked," recalled Gorman. At her suggestion, the LCW notified City Council that its "16,000 strong group" was considering asking for a royal commission inquiry into the CP plan.[22]

The Council of Women hosted an open meeting on June 10 at Central High School to investigate whether "democratic and moral principles had been compromised." Leaders of Calgary's religious denominations were invited to speak on "business interfering with our democratic process." Chaired by university chaplain Rev. John Paterson, and with well over 150 in the audience, including Aldermen Dave Russell, Walter Boote, Ernie Starr and Jack Leslie—all of whom opposed the CPR project—

the meeting voted to ask for an impartial judicial inquiry into influence exerted on civic employees and elected officials.[23]

"Escalating costs put the Plan out of its misery," concludes Norris. Relocating the Hudson Bay Company's warehouse west of 14th Street to allow for the parkway would cost the city $250,000; acquiring a right-of-way across CN property would cost a stupendous $5 million or more. Finally, when the mayor, three aldermen and chief city commissioner returned from a fruitless bargaining session at CPR head office in Montreal, they

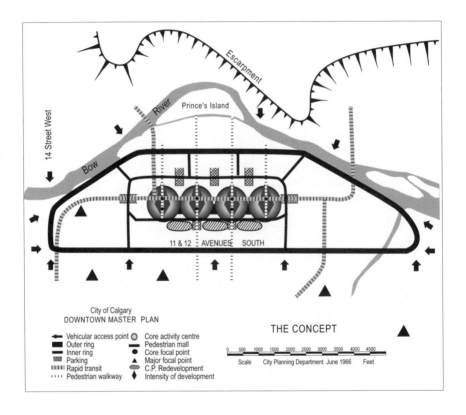

Planning Advisory Committee. The Future of Downtown Calgary. City of Calgary, 1966.

unanimously recommended that the agreement be dropped. On June 22, City Council supported them by a vote of ten-to-three.[24]

That same day, Council returned to its seemingly stillborn master plan for the city centre—the Downtown Plan, the high point perhaps of Calgary modernism. Downtown certainly needed attention. In 1964, it was estimated that approximately 40 percent of the city's labour force worked in the downtown area, but the resident population was a meagre two to three percent of the city total. And with the tremendous population growth of Calgary and the spread of the suburbs, downtown general property taxes had decreased from 31 percent of the total city in 1945 to 15 percent in 1965. [26]

Council's Planning Advisory Committee (chaired by

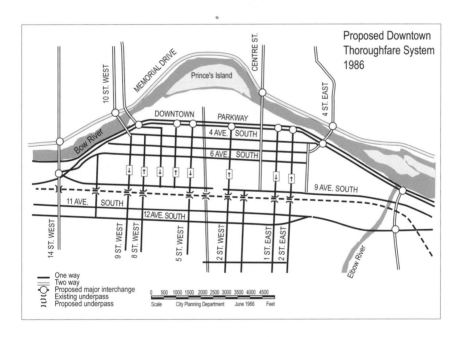

Planning Advisory Committee. The Future of Downtown Calgary. City of Calgary, 1966.

Mayor Jack Leslie and downtown map, 1966. (Glenbow Archives NA–3585–52)

Alderman Dave Russell) acknowledged that there was "very little in Downtown Calgary that is exciting or interesting; there is much that is drab and depressing." The committee especially mentioned the "lack of parks and breathing space," and the "slow rate of progress in obtaining public access to the banks of our Bow River." The plan promised an "interesting and exciting Downtown, elimination of old and worn-out parts, more open space and full public enjoyment of the Bow River."[27]

Yet the plan's "first objective" was to almost double the number of automobiles entering downtown over the next 20 years. This would be accomplished by a "network of limited access, high capacity roadways that feed into a downtown ring system which serves to collect and distribute traffic to its ultimate destination." Inside this high speed ring system would be an inner roadway network, "comprised of one-way couplets, that frames and protects the Core from intensive automobile penetration and gives direct connection with large parking structures." At the same time, an "H" configuration of rapid transit routes would feed Downtown, converging along 7th Avenue, offering an alternative to the automobile and reducing demand for parking space in the city centre.[27]

As the most significant feature of the Plan, the 8th Avenue Mall would link together the principal downtown components along an east-west axis: civic centre, retail core, financial core and office core. With vehicular traffic excluded from 8th Avenue, a series of "open plazas and squares, bounded by colonnades, arcades and malls," would provide a "pattern of great interest, creating a change of pace and atmosphere within the heart of Downtown." The east-of-Centre- Street skid row area would be replaced with an institutional and residential area known as Churchill Park, including a new library, school board offices, a junior college, a senior citizens' high-rise project, and medium and high-density residential buildings. Finally, in words that must have pleased the Local Council of Women, the riverbanks "should be an attractive backdrop to Downtown, a recreational area for the use of Downtown and city-wide residents, an attraction to visitors and a feature that, above all, is unique to Calgary."[28]

Unfortunately (or fortunately), not all aspects of the Downtown Plan were fully realized.

Churchill Park's $24.5 million urban renewal scheme stalled after its 38-acre first phase—school board offices, police station, public library—cleared most of eight city blocks and dislocated 475 area residents. But the other 90 acres—the East Village stretching east to the old Fort Calgary location—somehow did not get flattened and were only partially redeveloped with assisted-housing high-rises. Likewise, the proposed network of "limited

Jack Leslie and family. (Glenbow Archives NA–3585–24)

access, high capacity roadways" feeding into the core, including an east-west Downtown Parkway along a 2nd-3rd Avenue alignment, were never built. Like the previous CPR proposal, local opposition combined with escalating costs to scupper the most grandiose aspects of the Downtown Plan.

At the end of his term, Mayor MacEwan began his new career as Lieutenant Governor of Alberta, and Jack Leslie, the alderman who first opposed the Downtown Plan, was elected Calgary's mayor. In 1967, Leslie reminisced about the "year-long fight with the CPR" to keep the railroad off the banks of the Bow River. "The end result wasn't exactly what we wanted," he admitted, "but it was certainly a lot better than what the CPR proposed." We have "beautiful pathways and parks" along the river and Prince's Island. "It sure beats a dusty railroad track along the edge of the Bow."[29]

Beyond Modernism

"Modern," "modernism," and "modernist" are words that refuse to go away. We use them as synonyms for innovative, contemporary, pioneering, fresh, even design-conscious. Yet it is important to remember that while "modernity" may be a state of mind, both "modern" and "modernism" more properly refer to a historical movement in art and architecture, design and urban planning, living and enjoying life, that was confined to portions of the 20th century. Modernism made its full impact on Calgary in the 20–25 years following the Second World War. By the late 1960s and early 1970s, however, Calgary, in concert with most of urban North America, was slipping from modernism into postmodernism.

The symbolic death of North American modernism has been announced in the most definite and precise manner possible by American architect Charles Jencks. According to Jencks, this termination point occurred at 3:30 p.m., July 15, 1972, in St. Louis, Missouri, when the Pruitt-Igo public housing development—a clean-lined, rational, prize-winning piece of modernist architecture—was blown up with dynamite, destroying the ghetto which had "transformed the modern dream into a pre-historic nightmare." For Jencks and other observers, "all modernist aspirations seemed to collapse with the annihilation of these functional structures."[30]

Yet warning signs appeared long before this St. Louis detonation. In 1961, Jane Jacobs published *The Death and Life of Great American Cities*, a condemnation of postwar city planning and urban revitalization techniques. She argued that modern concepts such as superblocks, separation of land uses and destruction of entire neighbourhoods in the name of urban renewal destroyed the vitality of cities. Jacobs urged designers and planners to be more sensitive to the existing city fabric and more accepting of diverse functions and building styles. Five years later, in *Complexity and Contradiction in Architecture*, architect Robert Venturi advocated "complex and contradictory architecture based on the richness and ambiguity of modern experience," in which to live with contradictions. Theories about housing and urban planning, once held to be the very heart of modernism's special claim to ethical competence, by the end of the 1970s had been largely repudiated for contributing to the environmental dysfunctions they were supposed to end.

Several public buildings from mid-1960s Calgary illustrate the coldness of modernist architecture, while at the same time pointing the way to postmodernism. The new central branch of the Calgary Public Library, the administrative offices of the public and separate school boards, are all massive concrete structures, almost brutalist in form, lacking the lightness of Elveden Centre and earlier downtown modernist structures. The Centennial Planetarium of 1967 (now the Calgary Science Centre), has also been labelled "brutalist," combining "broad-formed, rough concrete … with forms that clearly allude to mediaeval castles." Yet another critic admires how the Planetarium's walls and ceiling "undulate in sculptural patterns, creating a lively organic space." Its "ever-

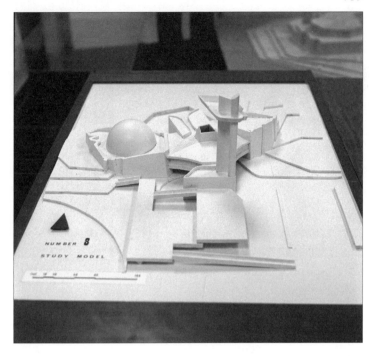

Calgary Planetarium model. (Glenbow Archives NA–2864–1454, 3b)

changing forms are stimulating, its functions are well organized, and spatially it points the way to the future."[31]

In contrast to the architecture that represented the mainstream of the Modern movement, postmodernist building addressed the individual rather than the mass, the personal rather than the anonymous, the unexpected rather than the sustained program of repetitive building types.[32] In his 1977 book, *The Language of Postmodern Architecture*, Christopher Jencks defined postmodernism as a hybrid style concerned with issues of historical memory, local context, metaphor and ambiguity. Endorsing "radical eclecticism" to allow a wider understanding

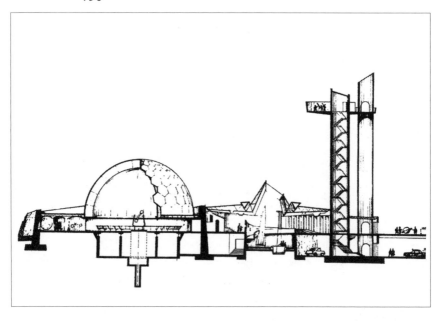

Calgary Planetarium section. (Glenbow Archives NA–2864–1454, top)

of the variety of human culture, he described postmodernism as pluralistic, "variegated rather than homogenous, witty rather than sombre, messy rather than clean, picturesque but not necessarily without a classical, geometrical order."[33]

Yet postmodernism was (and remains) more than just architectural in scope. It has much broader cultural significance, suggesting a more laid-back pluralism, a greater range of lifestyles.

Jack Long, who with partner Hugh MacMillan designed the Centennial Planetarium, is a key figure in nudging Calgary toward postmodernism. Architect, planner, community advocate, founder of The New Street Group and clearly in the Jane Jacobs mode, Long moved to Calgary from the eastern United States in 1960. He soon got involved in the Local Council of Women's fight over

Family of Man sculptures, 1968. (Glenbow Archives NA–3585–51)

the relocation of the CPR mainline through downtown along the edge of the Bow. "The plan would have had disastrous implications for the river and for inner-city communities," Long concluded.[34]

July 8, 1968, is perhaps the best date to signal Calgary's transition from the modern to postmodern age. That day, in a gala ceremony on the grounds of the Calgary Board of Education's new Education Centre complex, the city took possession of the Family of Man sculptures. Officially the Mario Armengol sculptures, these 10 aluminum figures commissioned for the British pavilion at Expo 67, had been purchased by developer Robert Cummings (Calgary Place complex, Pacific Petroleum Building) and donated to Calgary. "Standing 21 feet tall yet unmistakably human—

naked, raceless, expressionless, they extend hands in gestures of fellowship and goodwill," wrote Jean Leslie 26 years later.[35] By eschewing the solitary, heroic male and highlighting both the insignificance of the individual and the interdependency of the family, Armengol's sculptures provide a fitting symbol for postmodern Calgary.

Postmodernism condemned the authoritarian, imperialistic and chauvinistic aspects of modernism, and recognized new aspirations of diverse social currents, such as feminism and multiculturalism, and eventually gay and lesbian liberation. Postmodernism, claims Linda Hutcheon, "takes the form of self-conscious, self-contradictory, self-undermining statement," forcing society to re-examine basic tenets of capitalism, liberalism and patriarchy. For Hutcheon, postmodernism called into question the "messianic faith of modernism," the faith that "technical innovation and purity of form can assure social order." Postmodernism assumed an attitude "fundamentally demystifying and critical," and among the things it most criticized were "modernism's elitist and sometimes totalitarian modes."[36]

Postmodernism seems to have developed out of a reaction against the seriousness and elitism of high modernism. In an age of consumerism, it attacked the exclusiveness, the cultural pretensions of modernism. Postmodernism, claims John Jervis, functions as an ideology of popular culture, culture in the age of mass consumerism. It "proclaims the revenge of popular culture on the elitism of modernism." Furthermore, argues Jervis, if the project of modernity is in some sense "coded masculine," resting on and reproducing a certain "fixity in gender positions," then the postmodern could be seen either as the "revenge of the feminine" or even as a "de-differentiation or questioning of the gender boundary itself."[37]

Modernism as masculine, postmodern as feminine? Such a dichotomy may withstand scrutiny in the more formal, high modernist aspects of art, architecture and design; it may play out in the avant-garde neighbourhoods of New York and Paris. But in Calgary's case, where modernism went middle-class, down-market and decidedly suburban, we cannot neglect the important role of women in defining the movement. Certainly, the leadership taken by Calgary women in defeating the CPR track-relocation plan and modifying the Downtown Master Plan helps us understand not just the end of modernism, but also provides clues to understanding the nature of the modernist movement in this city.

Cultural critic Elizabeth Wilson helps explain the long-neglected yet important role of women and femininity in defining modernism. In her book *The Sphinx in the City*, Wilson points to crucial ways in which the experience of the 20th-century city was gendered, and suggests that women have in a sense been "an interruption in the city, a symptom of disorder, and a problem: the Sphinx in the city." While the city is "masculine in its triumphal scale, its towers and vistas and arid industrial regions," Wilson finds it "feminine in its enclosing embrace, its indeterminacy and labyrinthine uncentredness." She suggests that urban life is actually based on "this perpetual struggle between rigid, routinised order and pleasurable anarchy, the male-female dichotomy."[38]

Downtown masculinity and suburban femininity? The suburbs rather than downtown Calgary defined Calgary's particular approach to modernism. Calgary modernism was essentially middle-class rather than avant-garde. It was driven by mass consumerism rather than by iconoclastic individualism. It found its ideal manifestation in suburban bungalows and split-level houses, where proud first-time home owners showed off their modern furniture and labour-saving appliances while gazing out their picture windows at their shiny new automobiles. The aesthetic was suburban rather than urban—suburban modern.

Endnotes

Chapter 1: Waiting for the Modern Age

1 Hugh A. Dempsey, *Calgary: Spirit of the West.* (Saskatoon: 1994), 131.

2 *Ibid.,* 132.

3 *Calgary Herald,* 14 January 1947.

4 Robert J.C. Stead, "Calgary—"City of the Foothills," *Canadian Geographic Journal,* April 1948.

5 James Gray, "Calgary Celebrates," *The Beaver,* June 1950.

6 *Calgary Herald,* 4 August 1948 and 12 February 1945.

7 *Ibid.,* 5 June 1948 and 23 January 1953.

8 Kathleen M. Snow, *Maxwell Bates: Biography of an Artist.* (Calgary: 1993), 104.

9 *Calgary Herald,* 27 March 1945, 4 October 1946, 9 November 1946, 10 June 1948 and 8 July 1948.

10 *Ibid.,* 5 February 1948, 19 November 1949 and 30 March 1951.

11 *Ibid.,* 26 April 1949 and 15 July 1953.

12 Allan Collier, "Western Canada," in Robert McKaskell, ed., *Achieving the Modern: Canadian Abstract Painting and Design in the 1950s.* (Winnipeg: 1953).

13 Marshall Berman, *All That Is Solid Melts into Air: The Experience of Modernity.* (New York: 1982), 15-16.

14 John Wilson Foster, "Romantic Revival, Modernist Prescription," in Benjamin H.D. Buchloh, et al., eds., *Modernism and Modernity: The Vancouver Conference Papers.* (Halifax: 1983), 67.

15 Berman, *All That is Solid Melts into Air,* 24.

16 Suzi Gablik, *Has Modernism Failed?* (London: 1984), 16.

17 John Jervis, *Exploring the Modern: Patterns of Western Culture and Civilization.* (Oxford: 1998), 65-67.

Chapter 2: A Vertical Downtown

1 Max and Heather Foran, *Calgary: Canada's Frontier Metropolis.* (N.P.: 1982), 229.

2 David Breen, "Calgary: The City and the Petroleum Industry Since World War Two," *Urban History Review*, 2-77 (1977), 61.

3 Eric J. Hanson, *Dynamic Decade: The Evolution and Effects of the Oil Industry in Alberta.* (Toronto: 1958), 259-270.

4 Foran and Foran, *Calgary: Canada's Frontier Metropolis*, 236.

5 Breen, "Calgary: The City and the Petroleum Industry," 61.

6 G.H. Zieber, "Calgary as an Oil Administrative and Oil Operations Centre," in Brenton M. Barr, ed., *Calgary: Metropolitan Structure and Influence.* (Victoria: 1975), 81, 84; Max Foran, *Calgary: An Illustrated History* (Toronto: 1978), 107.

7 James Lorimer and Evelyn Ross, eds., *The City Book.* (Toronto: 1976), 148-49.

8 Zieber, "Calgary as an Oil Administrative and Oil Operations Centre," 103, 107.

9 Max Foran, *Calgary: An Illustrated History*, 162-63.

10 James H. Gray, *Troublemaker! A Personal History.* (Toronto: 1978), 214-17.

11 Howard and Tamara Palmer, *A New History of Alberta.* (Edmonton: 1990), 306.

12 Gray, *Troublemaker*, 214-15.

13 Trevor Boddy, *Modern Architecture in Alberta.* (Edmonton: 1987), 77.

14 *Calgary Herald*, 7 January 1950.

15 Boddy, *Modern Architecture in Alberta*, 77-78.

16 *Calgary Herald*, 5 February 1948.

17 *Ibid.*, 10 February 1949 and 30 March 1951.

18 Boddy, *Modern Architecture in Alberta*, 79.

19 *Ibid.*, 78.

20 *Ibid.*, 80.

21 Jane Kondo, "Workplace," in Geoffrey Simmins, ed., *Calgary Modern: 1947-1967* (Calgary: 2000), 29-30; David Down and Graham Livesey, "Modern Love," *Avenue* (May 1997), 28-29.

22 *Calgary Herald*, 12 August 1995.

23 *Ibid.*, 15 October 1960.

24 Boddy, *Modern Architecture in Alberta*, 82-83.

25 Kondo, "Workplace," 31.

26 Zieber, "Calgary as an Oil Administrative and Oil Operations Centre," 82-83, 109.

27 Kondo, "Workplace," 27, 31.

28 Ibid., 28.

29 Gerald Forseth, "Curator Statement," in Simmins, Calgary Modern, 10.

30 Leslie Maitland, et al., A Guide to Canadian Architectural Styles. (Peterborough, Ontario: 1992), 178.

31 Boddy, Modern Architecture in Alberta, 17.

Chapter 3: A City Built for Speed

1 Calgary Herald, 6 June 1945.

2 Colin Hatcher, Stampede City Streetcars: The Story of the Calgary Municipal Railway. (Montreal: 1975), 74-77.

3 Calgary Herald, 29 January 1946.

4 Hatcher, Stampede City Streetcars, 75.

5 Calgary Herald, 6 November 1946 and 2 June 1947.

6 Ibid., 24 August 1948.

7 Ibid., 30 December 1950; Hatcher, Stampede City Streetcars, 78.

8 Ibid., 9 May 1975; The Albertan, 8 May 1975.

9 Calgary Herald, 27 April 1959.

10 Ibid., 30 January 1962.

11 Ibid., 30 December 1963.

12 Ibid., 9 March 1957.

13 Richard P. Baine, Calgary: An Urban Study (Toronto: 1973), 82.

14 Calgary Herald, 26 November 1962.

15 Ibid., 6 September 1950.

16 Ibid., 15 June 1951.

17 W.D. Grant to E.C. Thomas, 18 November 1954. City Engineer's Correspondence, City of Calgary Archives.

18 Ibid.

19 Calgary Herald, 9 March 1957.

20 Donald G. Harasym, "The Planning of New Residential Areas—Calgary, 1944-1973," University of Alberta M.A. thesis, 1974, 115.

21 Ibid., 118-19.

22 Calgary Herald, 8 December 1947.

23 Ibid., 15 January 1949 and 16 July 1953.

24 Haddin, Davis & Brown, *Report: Proposed Bridge and Subway, Fourteenth Street West, City of Calgary, Alberta.* (Calgary: 1952), 7-8.

25 *Calgary Herald*, 7 December 1954.

26 *Financial Post*, 19 February 1955.

27 *Calgary Herald*, 4 January 1967.

28 J.I. Strong to Ethel Patching, 28 April 1950. City Engineer's Correspondence.

29 *Calgary Herald*, 12 December 1947.

30 *Ibid.*, 18 May 1948.

31 *Canadian Aviation*, September 1954.

32 City of Calgary. Planning Department, *Calgary: 1967.*

33 Marshall Berman, *All That Is Solid Melts into Air*, 167.

34 *Ibid.*, 168.

Chapter 4: The Postwar Dream House

1 *Calgary Herald*, 16 August 1947.

2 *Ibid.*, 27 January 1945.

3 Humphrey Carver, *Houses for Canadians.* (Toronto: 1948), 132.

4 *Ibid.*, 3, 18-22.

5 *Ibid.*, 134; *Calgary Herald*, 3 December 1947.

6 *Calgary Herald*, 28 August 1948, 1 September 1948 and 31 December 1949.

7 *Ibid.*, 11 December 1995.

8 *Ibid.*, 10 August 1995.

9 Foran and Foran, *Calgary: Canada's Frontier Metropolis*, 304, 339.

10 *Calgary Herald*, 1 October 1949.

11 Ken Schmaltz, "Bungalow of Dreams," *Avenue*, May 1996, 12-17.

12 Donald Wetherell and Irene Kmet, *Homes in Alberta: Building, Trends, Design.* (Edmonton; 1991), 264.

13 Thomas Hine, *Populuxe.* (New York: 1986), 48.

14 *Calgary Herald*, 2 June 1945.

15 *Ibid.*, 2 August 1950.

16 Wetherell and Kmet, *Homes in Alberta*, 264.

17 Hine, *Populuxe*, 53.

18 City of Calgary, Engineering Department, *Annual Report*, 1956-65.

19 Stephanie White, "Decade Houses," *Calgary Magazine*, September 1980, 60.

20 Jeremy Sturgess, "Home," in Simmins, ed., *Calgary Modern, 1947-1967*, 41.

21 *Ibid.*, 41-42.

22 Graham Livesey, et al, *twelve modern houses: From the Collections of the Canadian*

Architectural Archives. (Calgary: 1995), 33-35.

23 Hine, *Populuxe*, 52.

24 Doug Owram, *Born at the Right Time: A History of the Baby Boom Generation*. (Toronto: 1996), 77.

25 Hine, *Populuxe*, 64.

26 Owram, *Born at the Right Time*, 76; Cherie and Kenneth Fehrman, *Postwar Interior Design, 1945-1960*. (New York: 1987, ix.

27 Hine, *Populuxe*, 55.

28 Lynn Spigel, *Making Room for TV: Television and the Family Ideal in Postwar America*. (Chicago: 1992), 38-39.

29 Owram, *Born at the Right Time*, 76.

30 Wetherell and Kmet, *Homes in Alberta*, 227-28.

31 *Ibid.*, 228.

32 Sturgess, "Home," 43; *Calgary Herald*, 23 October 1953.

33 Wetherell and Kmet, *Homes in Alberta*, 273-74.

34 Sturgess, "Home," 42-43

Chapter 5: Through Suburban Sprawl to Seamless City

1 Wetherell and Kmet, *Homes in Alberta*, 253.

2 D.G. Harasym and P.J. Smith, "Planning for Retail Services in New Residential Areas Since 1944," in Brenton Barr, ed., *Calgary: Metropolitan Structure and Influence*, 161, 169.

3 *Ibid.*, 163

4 Donald G. Harasym, "The Planning of New Residential Areas—Calgary, 1944-1973" (University of Alberta M.A. thesis, 1974), 80.

5 Harasym and Smith, "Planning for Retail Services," 166-67.

6 *Ibid.*, 170-72.

7 Harasym, "Planning of New Residential Areas," 67.

8 City of Calgary, Engineering Department, *Annual Report, 1959*.

9 Harasym, "Planning of New Residential Areas," 119.

10 Wetherell and Kmet, *Homes in Alberta*, 256.

11 *Calgary Herald*, 7 October 1950.

12 *St. Andrews Heights News*, November 1989.

13 Audrey Miklos, *History of St. Andrews Heights, 1953-1978*. (Calgary: 1978), 6-7.

14 *Ibid.*, 2,7.

15 *Ibid.*, 4.

16 *Calgary Herald*, 5 November 1955.

17 Harasym and Smith, "Planning for Retail Services," 177.

18 Harasym, "Planning of New Residential Areas," 194.

19 Harasym and Smith, "Planning for Retail Services," 179, 186.

20 James Lorimer, *The Developers*. (Toronto: 1978), 85; Kenneth T. Jackson, *Crabgrass Frontier: The Suburbanization of the United States*. (New York: 1985), 239-40.

21 Harasym, "Planning of New Residential Areas," 201; Wetherell and Kmet, *Homes in Alberta*, 258.

22 George Nader, *Cities of Canada*, II, 345.

23 Foran, *Calgary: An Illustrated History*, 166.

24 Wetherell and Kmet, *Homes in Alberta*, 258.

25 City of Calgary, Engineering Department, *Annual Reports, 1959-66*.

26 *Calgary Herald*, 4 April 1998.

27 S.D. Clark, *The Suburban Society*. (Toronto: 1966), 64-65, 83.

28 Wetherell and Kmet, *Homes in Alberta*, 234.

29 David G. Bettison, et al, *Urban Affairs in Alberta*. (Edmonton: 1975), 125, 133.

30 Hendrikus Lourens Diemer, *Annexation and Amalgamation in the Territorial Expansion of Edmonton and Calgary*. (Edmonton: 1974), 206.

31 *Ibid.*, 264-74.

32 *Ibid.*, 359-62.

33 Dorothy Nielson, *Bowness: Country Homes and Amusements West of Calgary*. (Calgary: 1975), 363-66.

34 Diemer, *Annexation and Amalgamation*, 363-66.

Chapter 6: Living the Modern Life

1 *Calgary Herald*, 13 May 1953

2 Trevor Boddy, "Times of the Sign," *Avenue*, September 1997, 30-36; Boddy, *Modern Architecture in Alberta*, 85; F.W. Boal and D.B. Johnson, "The Functions of Retail and Service Establishments on Commercial Ribbons," *Canadian Geographer*, 9 (1965), 154-69; F.W. Boal and D.B. Johnson, "Nondescript Streets," *Traffic Quarterly*, 22 (July 1968), 329-44.

3 Boddy, *Modern Architecture in Alberta*, 85-86.

4 Victor Gruen, "Cityscape and Landscape," *Arts and Architecture*, September 1955, 18-19, 36.

5 James Lorimer and Evelyn Ross, eds., *The City Book*. (Toronto: 1976), 188.

6 *Calgary Herald*, 16 May and 10 December 1998.

7   Nader, *Cities of Canada*, II, 346-47.

8   *Calgary Herald*, 16 August 1947.

9   Robert M. Stamp, *School Days: A Century of Memories*. (Calgary: 1975), 100.

10 Owram, *Born at the Right Time*, 81.

11 Stamp, *School Days*, 101.

12 R. Douglas Gillmor, "Education," in Simmins, *Calgary Modern*, 33-34; Carol Moore Ede, *Canadian Architecture, 1960-1970*. (Toronto: 1971), 58.

13 Stamp, *School Days*, 98.

14 Alberta Department of Education, *Annual Report, 1943*, 9.

15 Alberta Department of Public Works, *Jubilee Auditoriums; Edmonton and Calgary, Alberta*. (Edmonton: 1957), 17.

16 *Ibid.*, 45.

17 *Ibid.*, 46.

18 *Ibid.*, 25.

19 *Calgary Herald*, 12 November 1998.

20 George Brybycin, *Calgary: The Sunshine City*. (Calgary: 1989), 43.

21 Morrison, *The Calgary Stampede*, 151.

22 Illingworth Kerr, *Paint and Circumstance*. (Calgary: 1987), 120.

23 *Calgary Herald*, 26 January 1953.

24 Christopher Jackson, *Marion Nicoll: Art and Influences*. (Calgary: 1986), 44.

25 *Calgary Herald*, 7 July 1979.

26 R. Douglas Gillmor, "Worship," in Simmins, *Calgary Modern*, 36-39.

Chapter 7: The Limits of Modernism

1   *Calgary Herald*, 12 August 1953.

2   *Ibid.*, 22 March and 23 April 1947; Howard Palmer, "The Black Experience in Alberta," in *Peoples of Alberta: Portraits of Cultural Diversity*. (Saskatoon: 1988), 389-90.

3   *Calgary Herald*, 11 March 1947.

4   Calgary Fire Department, *A Century of Firefighting: Milestones and Mementoes, 1885-1985*. (Calgary: 1985), 253.

5   Alison Prentice, et al., *Canadian Women: A History*. (Toronto: 1988), 307-08.

6   Veronica Strong-Boag, "Home Dreams: Women and the Suburban Experiment in Canada, 1945-60," *Canadian Historical Review*, 72:4 (1991), 471-74.

7   *Ibid.*, 479.

8   *Ibid.*, 492.

9   Jean Leslie, *Glimpses of Calgary Past*. (Calgary: 1994), 110-12.

10 *Calgary Herald*, 23 February 1998.

11 *Ibid.*, 28 March 1997.

12 Prentice, *Canadian Women*, 312; J.L. Granatstein, *Canada 1957-1967: Years of Uncertainty and Innovation*. (Toronto: 1986), 7.

13 Strong-Boag, "Home Dreams," 504.

14 Marjorie Norris, *A Leaven of Ladies: A History of the Calgary Local Council of Women*. (Calgary: 1995), 200.

15 *Calgary Herald*, 5 April 1963.

16 Norris, *A Leaven of Ladies*, 198-200.

17 *Ibid.*, 200.

18 *Ibid.*, 201-02.

19 *Ibid.*, 206.

20 *Ibid.*

21 *The Albertan*, 21 May 1964.

22 Norris, *A Leaven of Ladies*, 208.

23 *Ibid.*, 208-09.

24 *Ibid.*, 209.

25 Foran, *Calgary: An Illustrated History*, 163; City of Calgary, Planning Advisory Committee, *The Future of Downtown Calgary*. (Calgary: 1966), 16.

26 Planning Advisory Committee, *The Future of Downtown Calgary*, intro.

27 *Ibid.*, 5.

28 *Ibid.*, 5,7.

29 Norris, *A Leaven of Ladies*, 210.

30 Serge Guibaut, "The Relevance of Modernism," in Buchloh, *Modernism and Modernity*, ix-x.

31 Boddy, *Modern Architecture in Alberta*, 93; Ede, *Canadian Architecture*, 82.

32 Nuttgens, *Understanding Modern Architecture*, 2.

33 Charles Jencks, *Modern Movements in Architecture*. (Garden City: 1973), 92.

34 William Bernstein and Ruth Cawker, *Building with Words: Canadian Architects on Architecture*. (Toronto: 1981), 67.

35 Leslie, *Glimpses of Calgary Past*, 50.

36 Linda Hutcheon, *The Politics of Postmodernism*. (London: 1989), 1-2, 12, 26.

37 John Jervis, *Exploring the Modern: Patterns of Western Culture and Civilization*. (Oxford: 1998), 334-36.

38 Elizabeth Wilson, *The Sphinx in the City*. (London: 1991), 7-9, 25.

Suggestions for Further Reading

Alberta. *Royal Commission on the Metropolitan Development of Calgary and Edmonton.* Edmonton: Queen's Printer, 1956 (McNally Commission).

Alberta. Department of Economic Affairs. *Economic Survey, City of Calgary.* Edmonton: 1950.

Alberta. Department of Public Works. *Jubilee Auditoriums, Edmonton and Calgary, Alberta.* Edmonton: 1957.

Baine, Richard P. *Calgary: An Urban Study.* Toronto: Clarke, Irwin, 1973.

Barr, Brenton M., ed. *Calgary: Metropolitan Structure and Influence.* Victoria: University of Victoria, 1975.

Berman, Marshall. *All That Is Solid Melts into Air: The Experience of Modernity.* New York: Simon and Shuster, 1982.

Bernstein, William and Ruth Cawker, eds. *Building with Words: Canadian Architects on Architecture.* Toronto: Coach House Press, 1981.

Bernstein, William and Ruth Cawker. *Contemporary Canadian Architecture: The Mainstream and Beyond.* Toronto: Fitzhenry & Whiteside, 1982.

Bettison, David G., et al. *Urban Affairs in Alberta.* Edmonton: University of Alberta Press, 1975.

Boddy, Trevor. *Modern Architecture in Alberta.* Edmonton: Alberta Culture and Multiculturalism; Regina: Canadian Plains Research Centre, 1987.

Bothwell, Robert, et al. *Canada Since 1945: Power, Politics and Provincialism.* Toronto: University of Toronto Press, 1981.

Breen, David. "Calgary: The City and the Petroleum Industry since World War Two," *Urban History Review*, 2-77 (1977), 55-71.

Brybycin, George. *Calgary: The Sunshine City.* Calgary: GB Publishing, 1989.

Buchloh, Benjamin H.D., et al., eds. *Modernism and Modernity: The Vancouver Conference Papers.* Halifax: Nova Scotia College of Art and Design, 1983.

Calgary Herald. 50 Years of Black Gold: A Special Section. Calgary: 1997.

Calgary Power Ltd. *Alberta—Province of Opportunity.* Calgary: 1958.

Canada Mortgage and Housing. *Housing in Canada, 1945-1986.* Ottawa: 1987.

Carver, Humphrey. *Houses for Canadians.* Toronto: University of Toronto Press, 1948.

Carver, Humphrey. *Cities in the Suburbs.* Toronto: University of Toronto Press, 1962.

City of Calgary. *Metropolitan Calgary Population: Historical Review, 1946-1970.* Calgary: 1970.

City of Calgary. Engineering Department. *Annual Report, 1959-1967.*

City of Calgary. Planning Advisory Committee. *The Future of Downtown Calgary.* Calgary: 1966.

Clark, S.D. *The Suburban Society.* Toronto: University of Toronto Press, 1966.

Dempsey, Hugh A. *Calgary: Spirit of the West.* Saskatoon: Fifth House, 1994.

Diemer, Hendrikus Lourens. *Annexation and Amalgamation in the Territorial Expansion of Edmonton and Calgary.* Edmonton: 1974.

Ede, Carol Moore. *Canadian Architecture, 1960-1970.* Toronto: Burns and MacEachern, 1971.

Edwards, Arthur M. *The Design of Suburbia: A Critical Study in Environmental History.* London: Pembridge Press, 1981.

Fehrman, Cherie and Kenneth. *Postwar Interior Design: 1945-1960.* New York: Van Nostrand Reinhold, 1987.

Foran, Max. *Calgary: An Illustrated History.* Toronto: James Lorimer, 1978.

Foran, Max and Heather. *Calgary: Canada's Frontier Metropolis.* N.P: Windsor Publications, 1982.

Fraser, Sylvia, ed. *Chatelaine: A Woman's Place. Seventy Years in the Lives of Canadian Women.* Toronto: Key Porter, 1997.

Gablik, Suzi. *Has Modernism Failed?* London: Thames and Hudson, 1984.

Gilbert, James. *Another Chance: Postwar America, 1945-1968.* Philadelphia: Temple University Press, 1981.

Granatstein, J.L. *Canada 1957-1967: The Years of Uncertainty and Innovation.* Toronto: McClelland and Stewart, 1986.

Gray, James H. *Troublemaker! A Personal History.* Toronto: Macmillan, 1978.

Guimond, Pierre S. and Brian R. Sinclair. *Calgary Architecture: The Boom Years 1972-1982* Calgary: Detselig Enterprises, 1984.

Haddin, Davis & Brown Ltd. *Report: Proposed Bridge and Subway, Fourteenth Street West, City of Calgary, Alberta.* Calgary: 1952.

Hanson, Eric J. *Dynamic Decade: The Evolution and Effects of the Oil Industry in Alberta.* Toronto: McClelland & Stewart, 1958.

Harasym, Donald G. "The Planning of New Residential Areas— Calgary, 1944-1973." University of Alberta M.A. thesis, 1974.

Hatcher, Colin. *Stampede City Streetcars: The Story of the Calgary Municipal Railway.* Montreal: Railfare, 1975.

Hawkins, W.E. *Electrifying Calgary: A Century of Public & Private Power.* Calgary: University of Calgary Press, 1987.

Hilborn, James D., ed. *Dusters and Gushers: The Canadian Oil and Gas Industry.* Toronto: Pitt Publishing Company, 1968.

Hine, Thomas. *Populuxe.* New York: Knopf, 1986.

Hutcheon, Linda. *The Politics of Postmodernism.* London: Routledge, 1989.

Jackson, Christopher. *Marion Nicoll: Art and Influences.* Calgary: Glenbow Museum, 1986.

Jackson, Kenneth T. *Crabgrass Frontier: The Suburbanization of the United States.* New York: Oxford University Press, 1985.

Jackson, Lesley. *The New Look: Design in the Fifties.* London: Thames and Hudson, 1991

Jacobs, Jane. *The Death and Life of Great American Cities.* New York: Random House, 1961.

Jencks, Charles. *Modern Movements in Architecture.* Garden City: Doubleday, 1973.

Jervis, John. *Exploring the Modern: Patterns of Western Culture and Civilization*. Oxford: Blackwell, 1998.

Kennedy, Fred. *The Calgary Stampede Story*. Calgary: T. Edwards Thonger, 1952.

Kerr, Illingworth. *Paint and Circumstance*. Calgary: 1987.

Kroetsch, Robert. *Alberta*. Toronto: Macmillan, 1968,

Kwasny, Barbara and Elaine Peake. *A Second Look at Calgary's Public Art*. Calgary: Detselig Enterprises, 1992.

Leslie, Jean. *Glimpses of Calgary Past*. Calgary: Detselig Enterprises, 1994.

Livesey, Graham, et al. *twelve modern houses: From the Collections of the Canadian Architectural Archives*. Calgary: Aris Press and University of Calgary Press, 1995.

Lorimer, James. *The Developers*. Toronto: James Lorimer, 1978.

Lorimer, James and Evelyn Ross, eds. *The City Book*. Toronto: James Lorimer, 1976.

Lorimer, James and Evelyn Ross, eds. *The Second City Book: Studies of Urban and Suburban Canada*. Toronto: James Lorimer, 1977.

MacGregor, James G. *A History of Alberta*. Edmonton: Hurtig Publishers, 1972.

Maitland, Leslie, et al. *A Guide to Canadian Architectural Styles*. Peterborough: Broadview, 1992.

McKaskell, Robert, et al. *Achieving the Modern: Canadian Abstract Painting and Design in the 1950s*. Winnipeg: Winnipeg Art Gallery, 1993.

McKay, Ian, ed. *The Challenge of Modernity: A Reader on Post-Confederation Canada*. Toronto: McGraw-Hill Ryerson, 1992.

Miron, John R. *Housing in Postwar Canada: Demographic Change, Household Formation, and Housing Demand*. Kingston and Montreal: McGill-Queen's University Press, 1988.

Nader, George A. *Cities of Canada*. Toronto: Macmillan, 1975, 1976. Two volumes.

Naremore, James and Patrick Brantlinger, eds. *Modernity and Mass Culture*. Bloomington: Indiana University Press, 1991.

Nielsen, Dorothy. *Bowness: Country Homes and Amusements West of Calgary*. Calgary: Century Calgary Publications, 1975.

Norris, Marjorie. *A Leaven of Ladies: A History of the Calgary Local Council of Women*. Calgary: Detselig Enterprises, 1995.

Nuttgens, Patrick. *Understanding Modern Architecture*. London: Unwin Hyman, 1988.

Owram, Doug. *Born at the Right Time: A History of the Baby Boom Generation*. Toronto: University of Toronto Press, 1996.

Palmer, Howard and Tamara, eds. *Peoples of Alberta: Portraits of Cultural Diversity*. Saskatoon: Western Producer Prairie Books, 1988.

Palmer, Howard and Tamara. *Alberta: A New History*. Edmonton: Hurtig Publishers, 1990.

Peach, Jack. *A Shelter from the Winds of Illness*. Calgary: Foothills Hospital, 1990.

Peach, Jack. *The First Fifty Years: A Chronicle of Half a Century in the Life of the Calgary Real Estate Board, 1943-1993*. Calgary: Calgary Real Estate Boiard, n.d. (circa 1993).

Prentice, Alison, et al. *Canadian Women: A History*. Toronto: Harcourt, Brace, Jovanovitch, 1988.

Rose, Albert. *Canadian Housing Policies, 1935-1980*. Toronto: Butterworths, 1980.

Saarinen, Thomas F. "The Changing Office Functions in Calgary's Central Business District, 1946-1962." University of Chicago M.A. thesis, 1963.

Schwartz, Barry. *The Changing Face of the Suburbs*. Chicago: University Chicago Press, 1976.

Scollard, D. *Hospital: A Portrait of Calgary General*. Calgary: Calgary General Hospital, 1981.

Simmins, Geoffrey, ed. *Calgary Modern, 1947-1967*, Calgary: Nickle Arts Museum, 2000.

Smith, Donald B., ed. *Centennial City: Calgary 1894-1994*. Calgary: University of Calgary, 1994.

Snow, Kathleen M. *Maxwell Bates: Biography of an Artist*. Calgary: University of Calgary Press, n.d.

Sparks, Suzie, ed. *Calgary: A Living Heritage*. Calgary: Junior League of Calgary, 1984.

Spigel, Lynn. *Make Room for TV: Television and the Family Ideal in Postwar America*. Chicago: University of Chicago Press, 1992.

Stamp, Robert M. *School Days: A Century of Memories*. Calgary: Board of Education, 1975.

Strong-Boag, Veronica. "Home Dreams: Women and the Suburban Experiment in Canada, 1945-60," *Canadian Historical Review*, 72:4 (1991), 471-504.

Takla, Emile F. "Changes in Land Use Patterns in Downtown Calgary, 1953-1969." University of Calgary M.A. thesis, 1971.

Trouth, N.S. & A.L. Martin, "Land Development in Calgary," *Habitat*, 5, 3 (May-June 1962), 14-23.

Venturi, Robert. *Complexity and Contradiction in Architecture*. New York: MOMA, 1966.

Welin, R.A. *The Bridges of Calgary, 1882-1977*. Calgary: City of Calgary, 1977.

Wetherell, Donald and Irene Kmet. *Useful Pleasures: The Shaping of Leisure in Alberta, 1896-1945*. Regina: Canadian Plains Research Centre, 1990.

Wetherell, Donald and Irene Kmet. *Homes in Alberta: Building, Trends, Design*. Edmonton: University of Alberta Press, 1991.

White, Stephanie, "Decade Houses," *Calgary Magazine*, 3, 1 (September 1980), 55-64.

Whiteside, Leon. *Modern Canadian Architecture*. Edmonton: Hurtig, 1983.

Wilson, Elizabeth, *The Sphinx in the City*. London: Virago, 1991.

Wright, Robert. *The Economics of an Urban Renewal Scheme for the City of Calgary*. Calgary: Ried, Crowther & Partners Ltd., 1966.

Wright, Virginia. *Modern Furniture in Canada, 1920-1970*. Toronto: University of Toronto, 1997.

Robert M. Stamp, Ph.D., has enjoyed life and work as a high school teacher, antiquarian bookseller, and university instructor. He is the author of several books on Canadian history, including *Canadian Education: A History, The World of Tomorrow: A View of Canada 1939,* and *Royal Rebels: Princess Louise and the Marquis of Lorne.* He resides in Calgary and is a professor in the Faculty of Education at the University of Calgary.